Stepping Out

A Journey of the Soul

Kim Laliberte

Kim Laliberte
909) 518-8876

King's Agenda Publishing

Unless otherwise noted, all Scripture quotations are from the *New American Standard Bible ®*, Copyright © 1960, 1962, 1963, 1968, 1971, 1972, 1973, 1975, 1977, 1995 by the Lockman Foundation. Used by permission (www.Lockman.org)

Scripture quotations marked NLT are from the *Holy Bible, New Living Translation*, Copyright © 1996, 2004, 2007. Used by permission of Tyndale House Publishers, Inc., Wheaton, IL 60189. All rights reserved.

Scripture quotations marked NIV are from the *Holy Bible, New International Version ®*, NIV ® Copyright © 1973, 1978, 1984, 2011 by Biblica, Inc. ™ Used by permission of Zondervan. All rights reserved world wide. www.zondervan.com The "NIV" and the "New International Version" are trademarks registered in the United States Patent and Trademark Office by Biblica, Inc. ™

Scripture quotations marked KJV are from the *The Holy Bible, King James Version*

Book Cover Design: Sharon Holt; Internal Layout: John Laliberte
Cover Photo: Istock Photos, Sara Winter

ISBN:978-0-9977662-2-6 (softcover) Printed in the United States of America
ISBN:978-0-9977662-3-3 (E-book)

DEDICATION

To John: You are His gift to me. Your God-given gifts far outweigh mine. Thank you for walking this journey with me. You are the love of my life, and the one more than anyone who deserves credit for making this book happen. I love you.

To my son Jonathan: Your humor heals, your integrity speaks, and your commitment to God touches others. You are the Apple of His eye (and ours too). We love you.

To Jesus Christ, Savior, Soul Lover, Heart Seeker: You are the one Who sets the captives free, and I am free because of You. Thank You for letting me create with You.

ACKNOWLEDGEMENTS

As we walk this journey of life, we stand on the shoulders of those who have long gone before us, who are just a little bit ahead of us, or walking parallel journeys with us. We need each other because nearly everyone teaches us something. There are people, however, who God puts into our lives for a reason or a season to give us something specific. I offer my deepest gratitude and thanks for the *108 Prayer Team*. The first to join the team was Rebekah Pearce, who promised to *"pray for me and my family every day at 1:08 pm for six months"*. Fourteen others quickly followed suit: Dennis Gilbert, Connie Gilbert, Summer Dove, Richard Soikkeli, Karen Soikkeli, Kelly Cua, Charlene Humphries, Joann Albrecht, Joan Morrell, Pattie Sanchez, Nancy Salvato, Mary Jo Dell Imagine, Jan Hilton and Gayle Kott. I didn't choose you, you didn't choose you. God called you to this task because He knew you were faithful and He knew you would not give up on me. Thank you. You have been my lifeline.

There are others who assisted in the shaping of this book:

Mike Nelson, Bible Study leader and life-long learner. Thank you for your counsel and encouragement in reading Chapters 3-4

Bob Bishop, my amazing brother-in-law. Thank you for your help in reading the beginning chapters and helping me find my voice.

Connie Gilbert, for reading every page, checking every Scripture and encouraging me along the path to the end. You are an amazing friend and cheerleader!

Sharon Holt, beautiful soul. Thank you for stepping in to design an amazing book cover. If not for you, I might still be stuck.

Linda MacCubbin, my "Armor Expert" who spent countless hours helping to shape Chapters 19-21. The best words and ideas are yours. Thank you.

Victoria (Vicky) Eagleson. Your friendship through these many years runs through the tapestry of my life. I know you will see echoes of your words and encouragement in some of these pages. You have taught me much. Thank you.

Any doctrinal or other error is solely mine and cannot be laid at the door of any person who helped shape me or this book.

Kim Laliberte

TABLE OF CONTENTS

INTRODUCTION

"There isn't a need for more books. The world needs more books written by people who have been with God." -- Allen Arnold, Ransomed Heart Ministries

I love Walter Mitty. His story resonates with me. In the movie, *The Secret Life of Walter Mitty*, an ordinary man is the personification of a boring, uninteresting life. He is a man who is misunderstood, mistreated, ignored and almost invisible. When the "ping" to the girl of his dreams on social media fails to respond, even his geeky social media support guy feels sorry for him, suspecting a client who really has no life! *"Well, have ya done anything? Been anywhere?"*

Mitty spends most of his days in the basement of a major magazine he works for. His job as the magazine's photograph librarian is to catalog and protect the fruit of other people's dreams, people who actually are living out their fantasies. Mitty adopts these fantasies as his own, living his life through them. He has no life, no story. Or so it seems!

But, in truth, *everybody* has a story. Mitty's is lived out in his fantasy dream-life where the hero easily conquers every hardship. Every person who has ever looked askance at him or failed to see him somehow begins to see him for the hero he is and, of course, in the end, the hero always gets the girl.

When the most important photograph of his career is lost, Mitty is propelled on a journey to find the photographer, enabling him to actually *live out* the adventures he has only imagined. In the midst of the journey, he learns how to live life outside of the basement.

To my way of thinking, I have just described the Christian life. I saw in this movie the great adventure God desires to call each of us to experience. Unlike Mitty, who goes on the journey alone, we can move forward knowing we are never alone! Through this movie I was moved to evaluate my own life in the "basement." And I wanted more. Jesus said in *John 10:10*, *"The thief comes only to steal, kill, and destroy; I came that they [His sheep] might have life, and might have it abundantly."*

In some ways, I cannot relate to Mitty's empty life because I have a good life. I have been a believer since I was a teenager and have loved Jesus and served Him faithfully. I've had many opportunities to teach, speak, and lead others using the gifts He has blessed me with. Where I can relate to Mitty is his desire for *more* in his life. This is reflected in my life journal which I've kept since age fifteen. It contains many statements like, *"What IS the abundant life Jesus is talking about? Is this it? Or is there more?"*

Over the past several years, I have begun to explore the possibility of *more* – the adventure of walking *with* Him, not just doing things *for* Him, pondering questions like, *"Why haven't I experienced more joy, more miracles, more of everything His Word promises? Why wasn't I experiencing life outside the basement that others seemed to be enjoying? Why was I experiencing so few miracles in my life while the Bible states we should expect many (a lot more)? What was missing?"*

It turns out I was missing one very small piece in my thinking. It was something hidden in plain view that I had read many times in the Bible over the years but had somehow missed. It was the first part of John 10:10, *"The thief only comes to steal, kill and destroy..."* I don't remember ever reading it until recently – and *that*, for me, was the missing piece to the un-lived abundant life! As I began to search out the *whole meaning* of John 10:10, I began to see there was a reason I was still in the basement and not living the abundant life Jesus was actually calling me to live. Many believers get stuck here too. Our inability to experience "more" is due to things in our souls we are not aware of. Things that, like weeds masking as healthy plants, are buried in the soul. We are not aware of them, believing instead lies like, *This is just how I am; this characteristic is part of my make-up; I'm not that way!* This book will help expose those hidden areas so you can receive healing.

In this book I often speak about "the enemy of our souls" who is Satan, the devil, the accuser of the brethren. I call him simply *the enemy*.

One of the most important lessons I learned was that I was to be *a part of* the battle. I thought that when I became a Christian, God was going to fight my battles and I could just wait on the sidelines while He showed up and solved things. *That is NOT the believer's walk!* I write for (and in some ways from) the frozen soul. There are those of you who, like me, sit in church Sunday after Sunday, enjoying the sermon, liking the worship, loving the people but then walking out with a deep unsettledness, thinking: *"Is this it? Isn't there more?"*

As I grew, I learned that He has gone before me and has already secured the victory. He gives me the weapons to go in and take the victory, leading the way and fighting alongside me. That is a different way of seeing for me. He *does* fight my battles, but it is with His strength and power in and through me. It was as I *stepped up* that change began to happen. It is a completely different way of living the Christian life! As I did these things, my life began to shift and change. I began to see and to experience freedom. I wasn't afraid. I knew who I was and I knew Whose I was. That has made all the difference! And that journey is the basis of this book.

What catapulted me on the journey occurred during a time when I, without even being aware of it, stepped out of Jesus' footsteps and went my own way. There are two ways of looking at "stepping out". Some writers speak of stepping out as positive and faith-challenging such as when Peter stepped out of the boat to get to Jesus. (Matthew 14:28) I speak at it from a different perspective. We are called to follow in Jesus' footsteps. When we step out of those footsteps, it speaks of being in disobedience and, from my perspective, sin. That is how I saw my journey described in Part One of this book. Part Two of the book chronicles how God led me back, teaching me strategies and weapons of war. In the midst I experienced deep joy, peace and freedom that I had rarely experienced prior to this time. In this book I plan to give you as many of the tools as I have learned during that time to use in your own life.

This book begins with salvation. From there we will journey straight on through life into what it means to walk in Jesus' footsteps and we will learn to recognize what life outside the footsteps looks like.

This book may present some challenges to you in terms of how you see the Christian life. Many of my own beliefs were challenged as I walked this journey. We might explore things you disagree with. Some subjects may rub against your long-held beliefs. It is up to you how you choose to respond. For me, some of my long-held beliefs needed to change to get soul healing. I had to move outside of my comfort zone to get answers. I had to throw myself on God's mercy, and surrender what I thought I knew and believed to be sacred truth. I had to become solely dependent on God's Spirit and His Word to reveal the truth that I did not see or understand so I could obtain freedom. I am not a scholar. I do not claim to be a theologian, and I do not claim to be correct in every way. I am just telling you my story and how God began to heal me.

I will use my painful story of sin, blindness and disobedience as a teachable example. We will explore the concepts of forgiveness, pride, repentance, cleansing, obedience and more. By using my life and my journey as a template, I will show you how the enemy sneaks in to try and steal our birthright in Christ; how he legally gains the right to harass us; how he seeks to kill, steal and destroy what God has given us.

We will look at several Bible passages and many stories. Each time, I will ask you to stop reading this book and pick up the Bible. I am asking you to read each passage as though you have never seen it before. Be open to a fresh Word from Him. His Word is more important than reading *this* book. *That* Book is where change comes from. I may also ask you to ponder and interact with the passage to see how it speaks to your own life. There is a companion study guide available to help you interact more fully with the principles in this book. At several points in the book I stop and ask you to write out what you see, think or feel.

I will share with you the *weapons of war* that I am learning from the Scriptures and from other believers who are farther along in this journey than I am. We will use the microscopic lens to examine some Bible passages that have shifted the way I live and see. Together, as we unpack my story, I'll help you unpack yours so that you will gain insight into your true calling in Christ.

If you are expecting a dramatic story of an outward fall and restoration, where my sin is "out there" for all to see, you will be disappointed. You will not find it here. My story is of the inner journey, the wounded and frozen heart. That is the more common one among believers who have known Him or served a long time. I speak to leaders, considered strong in the faith by some, giants of the faith by others. I speak to all of you who are on the journey, especially to you Jacobs (Genesis 32:26) who will not let God go until He blesses you with freedom and wholeness. I speak to all of you who want "more" – a deeper walk with Jesus.

Questions to Think About Before You Begin

Before we begin the journey, let me ask you some questions, some of which I hope to explore with you in this book. I invite you to ponder, pray and consider how your soul would answer:

- Assuming you believe that God has more for your life than you are experiencing right now, why do you think you are not experiencing it?

- Are you feeling stuck in your walk with God, frustrated, unfulfilled, or have a vague dissatisfaction with the way you are living the Christian life?

- Are you willing to open and expose your heart to God's Spirit so He can reveal to heal, even if it is painful and challenging?

- Are you desperate enough to take the plunge if you knew God wanted to deliver you from negative thinking, life in the basement, lies, brokenness and things that keep you down?

- Are you willing to let go of deep, long-held thinking patterns, such as: *everything depends on you, you are alone on the journey, God does not care about the things that concern you, He does not speak or answer your prayers, or He does not really love you?*

- Would you be willing to go where God's Spirit leads even if it is outside of your personal comfort zone?

- Do you really believe Jesus can rescue you and restore to you what the enemy has stolen from you?

- Are you willing, if God reveals through His Word, to let go of some doctrines and beliefs that are not working for you?

- Are you willing to learn how to pray differently, seek differently, and follow differently, if He calls you to it?

- Are you willing to move off the sidelines into the game if God calls you to join Him there?

These are some of the hard questions I have I had to ask in my own life. The answers I came up with pretty much rearranged my life, changing everything! I cannot tell you if this book will help heal your brokenness or not. Making the changes talked about in this book is up to you working in cooperation with God's Holy Spirit, Who resides in you.

Introduction

I hope that even if there are parts of the book you disagree with, you will keep reading with an open mind. There are many strategies explored and lessons to learn as we walk this journey together. I have come from the place of believing God did not love me enough to do these things *for me*, to the place of seeing and experiencing His deep love for me and freedom in my soul that I never believed possible. I will walk this journey with you to help you see and experience His love for *you*.

When you get to the end of this book, my hope and prayer is that you will see this book as written by someone who has been with God. I deeply desire for you to walk deeper with Him. I'm not "there" yet. I'm on the journey too. I'm just, as the old saying goes, "one beggar sharing bread with another."

It will be wholly a work of God's Word through the Spirit of Jesus resonating in your own soul and calling you. You can trust me that the Word of God is wholly better than anything I can say. But you must be willing to **Do. The. Work.**.... as He leads you.

We are all part of the unfinished story. So, are you ready to step out of the basement? Let's move!

Kim Laliberte

San Diego, CA
February 2018

Primary References

In the writing of this book there are several helps references I used often. I am grateful for:

The Complete Expository Dictionary of Old and New Testament Words – William D. Mounce

Vine's Expository Dictionary of Old and New Testament Words – W.E. Vine

Expository Dictionary of Bible Words – Lawrence O. Richards

Unger's Bible Dictionary – Merrill F. Unger

The series by Spiro Zodhaites, Th.D: *The Complete WordStudy Old Testament* and *The Complete WordStudy New Testament*

The series by Spiro Zodhaites, Th.D: *The Complete WordStudy Dictionary of the Old Testament* and *The Complete WordStudy Dictionary of the New Testament*

Part One: Stepping Out – How We Step Out of Jesus' Footsteps

"The thief comes only to steal, and kill, and destroy; I came that they might have life, and might have it abundantly." -- John 10:10

Chapter 1. You were Meant for More

"I have come that they may have life, and that they may have it more abundantly." -- John 10:10b (NKJ)

"Over the margins of life comes a whisper, a faint call, a premonition of richer living which we know we are passing by. Strained by the very mad pace of our daily outer burdens, we are further strained by an inward uneasiness, because we have hints that there is a way of life vastly richer and deeper than all this hurried existence, a life of unhurried serenity and peace and power." -- Thomas Kelly, *A Testament of Devotion*

Looking for Life in All the Wrong Places

She carried the answer with her the whole time but she did not know it. The power to go home was available to Dorothy during every part of her journey to Oz but she was clueless on activating it. She spent most of her time in Oz seeking the wrong solution. When the house dropped on the Wicked Witch of the West, the Ruby Slippers became Dorothy's. The only warning she received was never to take them off for they, *"must be very powerful if her sister wants them so badly."* It was not until the very end of the journey, when the Wizard failed her and sailed away without her that Dorothy learned the truth: the Ruby Slippers were the key to getting home all along.

This story is not unlike some who trudge through the Christian life wondering why there is no power in their own life when the Bible is full of promises of overcoming power, joy, victory and a promise of abundant life. I know that feeling. I have been there. Perhaps you have too. But I am going to tell you right up front that there is more.

1

There *is* victory. There *is* joy. There is much, much more to this life than we have ever dreamed possible. The Bible says we are overcomers, not we can become or we might be overcomers. Emphatically, we *are* who He says we are and we need to learn how to live in that victory. Like Dorothy's power to go home, the power to live it has been within you from the moment you invited Jesus Christ into your life.

You were meant for this – abundant living. That is what Jesus said: *"I have come that you might have life and that you might have life more abundantly"*. If you are like me, you ascribe to the adage, *"God said it; I believe it; that settles it."* Okay, that's settled, so why am I not experiencing it? I have explored this concept over the years, wondering about it myself. Because of the pain of separation I was experiencing from God, I began a desperate search for a way back. Surprisingly, after poking around in some dusty books that have been sitting on the library shelf for years, I think I have some ideas about it. What I found was not what I expected.

I bought into the preaching and testimonies that told me when I came to Christ I would have an abundant life full of peace, joy, and love. It was more of a lifestyle of what He could do for me rather than who He is. And, to some extent, I have experienced all that and more. But honestly, I have always had a sneaking suspicion that there really *was* more than I was experiencing. I wanted *more of Jesus*, not just a better life on the outside. I wanted a deeper walk, more fullness, more depth, more Spirit. I was greedy with desire for more abundance and more of Him in my life. I knew I was meant for more but I did not know how to find it. And I am not alone. As I have talked with people and spoken to groups at churches, retreats and luncheons, I have repeatedly heard the cry for more. People were asking me the same questions I was asking God and myself.

As I am writing this, I have on my desk a list of nineteen people who are studying my *Acts Project* book. I asked the leader to send me a list with one prayer request from each person: *"I want to be led by the*

Spirit." "I want to be closer to God." "I want to hear Him more." "I desire a deeper relationship with Him." "I want to love Him more." "I want to heed Him when He calls." Yep! I'm not the only one. So, what does it mean, this promise called *abundant living?*

Let the Bible Explain It

I think the best place to start is by looking at the parable or story where Jesus' actual words are used. Before I do this, however, I want to encourage you to go to the actual Scriptures to read the verses I write about. *Those are the inspired words. Those are the words that can change you forever. My words can only lead you to the well. You have to choose to drink from its healing waters.* And every time I ask you to read a passage, I want you to stop and pray. Ask the Holy Spirit (the Spirit of Jesus), Who is our Teacher, our Guide and the One who leads us into all truth, to speak to your soul. Even if you think you have not heard anything, I want you to exercise faith and believe that His Word never comes back empty and will at some point take root (Isaiah 55:11-12). We will explore the concept of why the words of the Bible fail to take root in your soul at a later point in the book.

According to William Hendriksen[1], a parable is *"an earthly story with a heavenly meaning."* In John 10:1-18 we encounter the parable of the Good Shepherd. Listeners in Jesus' day understood sheep and shepherds since it was common to see shepherds herding their sheep into and out of the fold (sheep pen), heading toward green pastures for rest and restoration. Let's stop here and read the parable found in John 10:1-18.

In telling the parable, Jesus spoke of robbers and thieves who do not enter into the sheepfold by way of the door, but some other means (John 10:1). It is interesting and, of course, significant that Jesus distinguishes between robbers and thieves. A *thief* is one who comes in by stealth to steal a treasure. The Greek word is *kleptes.* We get the word "kleptomaniac" from this root word. A *robber* (Greek *lestes*)[2] is one who creates rebellion or insurrection.

So we learn that the thief comes to steal by stealth and the robber comes to stir up the sheep to rebel against the shepherd. Jesus was speaking to (and about) the Pharisees and leaders of the day, but there are always layered meanings to the stories in the Scripture, which make the words timeless and applicable to every life in every generation. We will look at this concept in more depth later in the book, but for now, think about this from the concept of the enemy sneaking in to our lives, trying to steal what is ours through faith, and attempting to incite us to rebel (commit sin, step out of Jesus' footsteps) against the Shepherd.

Jesus, in further explaining the parable, tells His listeners that He is the Door by which the sheep enter (10:9) *and* those who choose to go in through the Door will be saved and find pasture. Jesus is the Door to every blessing in the believer's life. Every opportunity God gives us comes from walking in His way, through His Door. Think job opportunity, living situation, promotion, ministry opportunity, healing. We also learn from this parable that Jesus is the Good Shepherd who lays down His life for the sheep (10:11). Between verses nine and eleven comes a verse that most believers have heard, most certainly taken out of context, and may not understand fully. That group included me.

Let's look carefully at John 10:10. We're going to get to the first part of that verse later, but for now let's just look at the second part, *"I have come that they may have life, and that they may have it more abundantly."*

- "I have come that they [His children] might *have*…" The Greek word *have* is *Echo*. It means, "To have; to hold on to; to wear; to possess." [3] With those possible meanings in mind, read John 10:10 again using some of those definitions. What do you see? *"I came that you might hold on to…" "I came that you might wear…" "I came that you might possess…"* What does this say to you about how you *have* abundant life? What would it look like in your life?

- "I have come that they might have *life...*" The Greek word *life* in this passage is *Zoe*. It means "life in the spirit and soul." It does not mean *physical life* (the Greek word *bios*). *Zoe* expresses all the highest and best that Christ is and which He gives to His own. It means life at the very highest level! This is a new approach for me. The abundant life Jesus meant for us to have takes place in the spirit and soul![4] It does not say, "*I will never get fired from my job, I'll never have pain or problems, I'll never experience financial loss, physical loss, I'll never suffer.*" It says I will have abundance in my soul and spirit and that abundance will help me stand firm in other areas. Beloved, abundant living comes out of the soul. When the soul is healthy, the rest of life is in balance, and we experience abundance or more in all areas of life. **That's different!**

- Finally, let's look at the last word, *abundant.* You will like this one. In the Greek it means, "superabundantly, over and above, extraordinary." It means, "*Spiritual blessings greater than any that have ever been communicated to man; all of the super-added things to make life blessed and happy.*"[5]

You and I are called to live out life at the very highest level! If we are missing out on experiencing life with these wondrous adjectives, we may be missing out on the best part of the believer's life!

Let's put it all together: "*I Jesus have come that you might possess, hold on to, wear life in the soul and spirit so that when your spirit and soul are healthy, you will experience all the highest and best which I give to My own; and that you will experience an extraordinary, overflowing, over and above spiritual life, greater than you have ever experienced.*" Wow. I'm in!

Here is the problem I experienced: I was looking for and expecting to live a victorious physical external, successful life on the outside without considering the necessity of having to care for the inner life of the soul and spirit.

The Scripture teaches that our lives are made of body, soul and spirit. There is a division among scholars whether we are *bipartite* which means body and soul (which includes the spirit) as two parts or *tripartite* which means body, soul and spirit, three parts. We don't need to get into this issue here. It is not an issue that should divide the believing community. I personally, through my own study, believe we are body, soul and spirit. (*Hebrews 4:12*)

Our spirit is where the Holy Spirit takes up residence when we put our faith in Christ. It is from there that we commune with Christ. It is His base of operation from which He begins the transformation of the soul. The soul consists of our mind, will and emotions – the part where sanctification occurs. It is where the 'becoming like Him' takes place. Craig von Busek explains that, "*...soul and spirit are mysteriously tied together and make up what the Scriptures call the heart.*"[6]

The key to understanding why you are not experiencing the abundant life is to understand that the soul is not automatically changed the moment you accept Christ. Traumas, wounds, hurts and things from the past do not just disappear. Remember all the baggage we bring with us? It is resident in the soul. Over time, as we receive more freedom, our minds are renewed and our souls are freed. The body is sort of like our outerwear. It clothes our soul and spirit.

Our souls are a vast, uncharted continent waiting to be explored. Our involvement with God's story, which comes from the depths of our soul and spirit, is the ultimate reason for life. God wants to take us on a journey to the interior. On this sanctification journey there will be mountains and valleys, peaks and rivers, beauty and badlands, and we will explore them with One in Whose footsteps we seek to walk. We will walk with One who has already been there and experienced all there is to know and more. Your journey will be different from mine and every other person who has ever lived. No two journeys are ever alike, just as no two snowflakes are never exactly the same.

Throughout my life, I have been and still am seeking God's healing in my soul from the wounds, pain and traumas of life that kept me down. But my definition of *abundant living* was skewed and I think a lot of us get stuck right here. I needed to pay attention to the soul and spirit first and, out of caring for that, the rest would follow. Do you see?

It is easier to see what life *outside* the footsteps of Jesus looks like when you understand this concept of what living *in* the footsteps of Jesus looks like. Kingdom Living is a work from the inside out. Jesus says in Matthew 6:33, *"But seek first His Kingdom and His righteousness and all these things shall be added to you."* My first book, The Call to Follow Jesus, Studies in the Gospel of Mark, explains it this way: *"A kingdom implies a ruler whose will is the rule of the kingdom. It's that simple. Either He is in charge as He lives out His rule in me, or I am in charge and set up my own kingdom in opposition to His."* A simple way to understand this concept is to ask yourself, *"Am I in the Christian life because of what God can do for me to make my life better or am I on this journey because of who Jesus is and what He did for me on the Cross?"*

In the next chapter we will consider three lifestyles of the believer to help us begin to unravel more about life in the soul. There is so much abundance and healing to be had!

Chapter 2. Experiencing the More You were Meant for

"Now to Him who is able to do exceeding abundantly beyond all that we ask or think, according to the power that works within us, to Him be the glory in the church and in Christ Jesus to all generations forever and ever. Amen" – Ephesians 3:20-21

"If you wish to live richly, deeply and spiritually you must cultivate the 'world within.' It is a thrilling world…with the Heavenly Father as our companion." – John T. Benson, Jr.

Three Ways of Experiencing the Christian Life

Many of us, even after we trust Christ, do not understand what it really means to follow Him. We thought life would be different than it is. We just know that one day (we do not even remember when) we stopped singing; we stopped enjoying God; we stopped serving, at least in our hearts; and, dare I say it?, some of us have stopped loving. Maybe outwardly we are still in step with the church culture but there is no longer any joy in the Christian life. No abundance. No sweetness. And we have no idea what happened or when it happened. Somewhere along the line we lost our joy, our purpose and, most importantly, our freedom. Like the proverbial lobster in a pot, the loss has been so slow, so subtle, and so incredibly devilish that we hardly noticed. I have wondered about that too. *Why does it happen? How does it happen?*

I have tried several ways of living the Christian life in the hope of restoring the lost joy, purpose and freedom. First, I experienced Christianity in my young life as what I call the *superwoman lifestyle*.

> *"I can do it all! I can be a Godly woman, keep my house spotless, serve my husband, raise my son, homeschool, work at the church, teach law, practice law, eat healthy and exercise. Oh, and, love God with all my heart, soul, mind and spirit while I'm at it."*

Uh … no! Slowly, almost imperceptibly, I was being robbed of the joy I first had, the love that was so amazing; the beauty that first drew me toward Him.

I have learned you cannot approach the Christian life like a self-improvement program. When you fail to keep all the balls in the air, when you do not obey every rule or do every job you think you have been given, you will beat yourself up, blame yourself and try harder. And you will fail again and again until you get tired of failing and want to walk away. I remember one day when life was pressing in on me with all the obligations I had taken on that I became overwhelmed. I put my head down on my desk and wept. *"I can't. I can't do this life anymore. Either You, God are there and can help me or You're not."* And slowly, over a period of years after that break, God began to gently woo me away from that lifestyle into His *plan*, His *path*, His *purpose*. God enables us and empowers us to fulfill His purposes, not ours.

Secondly, I have learned we cannot experience the abundant life by *pushing through*. I've seen people who stoically trudge through the Christian life, serving in the church, looking and sounding great outwardly, always smiling, but are inwardly hurting and limping along. An incongruent disconnect exists somewhere in the soul. They help others, arrive before the church doors open, and faithfully read their Bible hoping to find the silver bullet that leads to the abundant life. They hope things will change, but they don't, and they wear themselves out trying to please people and look the part of the happy, fulfilled Christian.

These people rarely complain about their inner struggles, inadequacies, disappointments and exhaustion. You might look at them and think they are "super Christians," but in reality they are leading, as Henry David Thoreau said, *"quiet lives of desperation."* I have personally lived the push-through "Christian" lifestyle. It failed for me too because it does not produce genuine change. The true Christian life is a process of regeneration, a work of a Holy, Almighty God. Only He can change us from the inside out and this only occurs with our cooperation and complete surrender.

Finally, there are the *wholly oblivious.* They are not even aware that their soul needs regenerating. Reading this material with incredulity, they would say, *"What is she talking about?"*

Illustrating this, I remember speaking to a group about how God exposes lies in our lives when we open up to receiving more of His Presence in our souls, more light, more healing, less negativity, less darkness. I said that we were all broken and need His intervention and healing. Afterward a woman I knew fairly well came up to me and said, *"I am not broken and do not have any of those problems you were speaking of. I am totally free."* Knowing she wasn't I felt an immediate compassion for her because I had been there too. She was not intentionally ignoring things. She, like me, did not know. She could not see the truth about the darkness in her soul. Like her I had thought, since I was a believer, everything was supposed to be fine. But it wasn't fine. I was tired, discouraged and joyless and I could not admit it, even to myself.

We all come to Christ with baggage in tow. Baggage does not show up one day to weigh us down. It comes from a soul that has been wounded, planted in our lives early on by disappointments, traumas, broken trust, fear, anxiety, poor choices and pain. When we unwittingly open the door to the traumas that overwhelm us, the enemy sneaks in and finds a toehold. If not dealt with, this toehold can become a foothold, a stronghold, and finally a stranglehold. We will talk about this more later.

Letting Go

My premise is that those of us who fit these lifestyles have not experienced all that "salvation" has to offer. We might understand the theology of salvation, that we have been saved from the penalty of sin and death (knowing we're going to heaven), but fail to understand that salvation is so much more. Besides heaven, the Savior's sacrifice gives us the means to overcome the *power* of sin and the snare of the enemy in our lives now. Most of us have not experienced the fullness of salvation even though that is the primary reason God sent His Son.

Learning how to get rid of that baggage is part of Jesus' war training. You do not get rid of these things by ignoring them or, like a weed, lopping off the top hoping it won't grow back. You have to deal with the roots. It is the only way to get free and that too is part of Jesus' training. That is part of what this book is about.

Isaiah 61:1-4 contains a snapshot of Jesus' job description. From it we learn that God sent Jesus to bind up the brokenhearted, free the captives, heal the blind (spiritually and physically), comfort all who mourn, and make beauty out of ashes. Does any of this describe your life? It certainly speaks to mine!

Stop here and read Isaiah 61:1-4 in your Bible. Jot down any insights it gives for your personal journey. Which of the things set forth in the Isaiah passage touches your life the most right now?

Our Misconceptions

One misconception that many of us buy into is that we do not need church or anyone else to help us with the Christian life.

I am a strong proponent of church. I believe every believer should be a part of a thriving church. It is where, as my friend Mickey Martin says, *"Together we are walking each other home."* I served in an amazing church with the most wonderful people and pastors. I deeply love and respect the Senior Pastor, Mark Hopper, who walked us through every crisis. But while we live together and serve together with others, we must place our total dependence on God to take us through. Sometimes His Spirit will lead us to healing through the offices of the church and sometimes He will take us a different path toward healing. We must be prepared to walk the way He leads. My journey began in the church I served and when we moved out of the area, it continued through different venues.

We also buy into the premise that all we have to do is to "get saved". The rest is up to God and we wonder why He doesn't help when things go wrong:

> *"Where is He when things begin to fall apart in my life? Why are all these things happening? How come He answers others' prayers and not mine? Why can't I seem to move forward? Why do I feel like I always come back to the same place of stuckness?"*

When we get to this place, we lose heart because we fail to understand the plan.

Take note of this: There is a reason why over a third of the Bible speaks about wars, battlegrounds, overcoming the enemy, gaining territory, putting on armor and being ready. God's Word gives us strategies for living. Every battle the Israelites fought in the Old Testament is more than just a history lesson. It is a boot-camp strategy given to us by God Himself. The truth is, we cannot sit back and expect our re-born spirit to change without stepping up to seek and search out God's plan for us. And I am not talking about a works mentality or a legalistic lifestyle. John the Baptist in Matthew 3:7-9 was telling the Pharisees the same thing:

> *"But when he saw many of the Pharisees and Sadducees coming for baptism, he said to them, 'You brood of vipers, who warned you to flee from the wrath to come? Therefore, bring for fruit in*

keeping with repentance; and do not suppose that you can say to yourselves, 'We have Abraham for our father...'"

In other words, you cannot sit back on your expectation that because you are born of Abraham, you will draw near to God. You cannot sit back on your expectation that because you at one point in life placed your trust in Christ, that you will have a close, deep walk with Jesus and you will have an abundant life with Him.

Indeed, you are the special, unique *beloved of God* and a citizen of His Kingdom. You have a purpose to fulfill *with Him* that you can miss if you try to sit out on the sidelines and expect your battles to be fought without you. You will get your "fire insurance," but you will not understand or experience the abundant life of which Jesus speaks. It has taken me a very long time to understand and embrace this concept. I am speaking about a Spirit-led journey full of God appointed lessons and battle strategies. It is a whole different way of living than I have ever lived.

I am indebted to my dear friend, Victoria Eagleson, for pointing this out to me as I whined to her about my journey. She told me to stand up and fight for more territory, to move out and not expect God to do for me what I was not willing to do with Him. Thanks, Vicky!

Tell Me More

When you placed your faith and trust in Christ, whether you knew it or not, your world shifted. I expected it, I watched for it, and I was disappointed when neither I nor those close to me saw it in me. When I accepted Christ, the very next day I asked my friends, *"Am I different? Do you see any change in me? Am I nicer? Huh? Huh? Huh?"* They did not see a difference and, sadly, I didn't either. I was sixteen. Many people get stuck right here: *It didn't work. I guess it's not true.* But that did not mean I was not different. The enemy's first volley in my life as a believer could have stopped me in the journey right there. Staying with it and taking God at His Word, I later learned,

"Therefore if anyone is in Christ, he is a new creature; the old things passed away; behold, new things have come." 2 Corinthians 5:17

It is a promise that is not dependent upon what we see or do not see, or how we feel or do not feel. As a new believer, God's Spirit began His work in me and gradually the way I saw the world began to change. I began to see life as He sees it. It is a work of the soul and, if we fail to do the soul work and pay attention, we could miss it.

It has taken me years to learn how to see people as God sees them. In fact, it is still a struggle to see some people that way, if you know what I mean. Eventually I began to see my world, and that of others, in bondage to a merciless tyrant who comes to, "...steal, kill and destroy." I began to understand that there really is a battle for the souls of men. But it is not an equal battle -- not like the "force" in *Star Wars*, where good and evil battle on equal territory. In *this* battle, there is a clear winner – no equality, no question. God is in charge. God wins. But the enemy wants us to think the stakes are even. It is a battle of the cosmos, and humanity is the prize. God's plan was to send His Son, a merciful Savior to deliver, rescue, save and make whole any and all of those who respond to His call. God calls us for fellowship with Him, creativity, abundant life and so much more. The first step in experiencing the abundant life is what the Bible calls *salvation*.

Salvation is Not Just About Where We Spend Eternity

The most familiar verse used to explain salvation is John 3:16:

"For God so loved the world, that He gave His only begotten Son, that whoever believes in Him should not perish, but have eternal life."

That's it, isn't it? The purpose of salvation is to have eternal life? Yes, but so much more. Putting your trembling faith in Christ back at the beginning of your Christian journey is the "being" part of the story. When that happens, instantly something changes *in our spirit* as His

15

Spirit comes to live in us. We become a dwelling place for His Spirit (1 Corinthians 6:19). Even if we do not feel differently, we can know it is by faith that we are saved (Ephesians 2:8, 9). We belong to Him eternally. We're in!

The "becoming" or maturing part happens *in our soul*, which is made up of our mind, will and emotions. It is also the seat of the heart. In Proverbs 4:23, Scripture tells us to, "*Watch over your heart with all diligence, for from it flows the springs of life.*" When God's Word speaks of the heart, it is telling us something about our soul, where all the wars, traumas, hurts and pain happen. The *NIV Study Bible* puts it this way:

> "*Heart. In Biblical language the center of the human spirit, from which springs emotions, thought, motivations, courage and action – the wellspring of life.*"[8]

These are the things God's Spirit in us wants to move in to heal. The more we cooperate and allow Him in, the more room is made in our soul for His blessings and abundance.

Think of it this way: We have already talked about the soul (heart) being like a large continent. Let me give you a graphic illustration: North Korea has been called "the dark continent" by some. Looking at it from space at night, it is the darkest place on the planet. There is almost no light in that part of the world, while the rest of the world shows large points of light.

Now, picture your soul with spaces filled in with dark space and light space. The dark spaces represent the unhealed traumas, hurts, and wounds from others. It also includes the attitudes, bad habits, addictions and other things that have happened to us or we developed throughout our lifetime. It can include our own choices, our sins, the actions of others, and generational wounds that have come on us. Some areas are dark and we do not even know why. We are largely ignorant of that fact. This is where the enemy can gain space from which to do his evil work in our lives. Francis Frangipane in his book, *The Three Battlegrounds* puts it this way:

"Many Christians debate whether the devil is on the earth or in hell; can he dwell in Christians or only in the world? The fact is, the devil is in darkness. Wherever there is spiritual darkness, there the devil will be." [9]

So, the enemy attaches to our darkness. It is why it can be so difficult to move forward in life. The light space in our souls represents the beauty, joy, good things, blessings received from others. They include gifts that have increased our joy, answered prayer, Scripture verses and principles that have taken root. You get the idea. As the light of Christ is invited into the darkness of our souls, He challenges and removes the things in us bringing darkness.

For some of us, our hearts can be a dark and uninviting place, a place we never want to go to. We will go anywhere; do anything, just to escape the pain. We look for love and healing in all the wrong places: a relationship, parties, alcohol, negative thinking, drugs, affairs, and astrology, even hurting ourselves or hurting others. Yet, as we allow the Holy Spirit access to our soul through surrender, repentance and cleansing, He begins to bring more light. Healing takes place little by little. And as the light increases, it dissipates or removes the darkness. As the light becomes stronger and brighter, our soul becomes freer. I have seen it happen. I have experienced it myself. I am convinced He reveals to heal.

Beloved, changing this part of you takes a lifetime and it is not something you can do alone. Scholars, pastors and those in the know call it *sanctification.* It is the process by which we are made holy. We are called to reflect His holiness in a dark and dying world. It is an internal state of being called forth through the Spirit of Jesus in us. It happens primarily in the soul. It is a work of God with us. All of us as believers are on the sanctification journey, but many of us fail to see or understand the genesis of the darkness in us. We do not know what to do to replace it with it with the light.

Exploring the Full Meaning of Salvation

The word *salvation* does not go away once we accept Him. It is still with us in a myriad of different ways. In 2 Corinthians 7:10 Paul tells the *believers*, *"Godly sorrow brings repentance that leads to salvation..."* (NIV). The implication here is that believers who are already saved need to repent in such a way that leads to salvation – or healing, restoration, wholeness.

The full meaning of the word comes to life as we walk the journey with Jesus. Our English language seems almost one-dimensional when put alongside the original languages of the Bible (Hebrew, Greek and Aramaic). One of the Greek words for salvation is *sozo*. It expands our understanding of salvation in a huge way. It provides the *"more"* we experience on the journey. It is the *"exceeding abundantly beyond"* of Ephesians 3:20.

Consider these other meanings from the Greek words for salvation:

> *"to heal, to rescue, to recover, to restore, to deliver, to preserve, to keep safe, to keep from destruction, to make whole."* [10]

These words imply journey! My friend Deanna Allen says it this way: *"Sozo means to deliver. To be saved or rescued out from under Satan's power and restored to wholeness or God's order and wellbeing."* [11] This is the "more" we were meant for: to experience more of His life now – not waiting for heaven.

As you read this book, you will undoubtedly see yourself in some of my journey and I want to encourage you, when things come up in your own spirit, to stop and communicate in prayer with God about these things. Do not rush through the principles laid out in this book. My journey is only a framework to teach you principles for your journey.

I recommend that you invest in the companion study guide to this book and a notebook to write things down. Let Him speak to you, let Him take you back to the places where hurts took root so the whole meaning of salvation can be applied. Learn how to apply the Scriptural principles and tools you will learn in this book. I will give you lots of guidance and personal examples. You will find examples from Scripture and tools to help you along the way. I'm in this life for a deeper walk with Jesus and, along the way, to obtain His promises of healing and abundant living. I want to bring as many of you who want the same things along on the journey.

You might even consider going through this book with a group of trusted friends. Beloved, we were meant to live life abundantly. Jesus came to set the captives free, so let's put on our helmet of salvation (Ephesians 6:17), don the ruby slippers, click our heels together, and move out!

Chapter 3. The Binding Chains

"God, be merciful to me, a sinner." -- Luke 18:13

"The very word, sin, which seems to have disappeared, was once a proud word. It was once a strong word, an ominous and serious word...but the word went away. It has almost disappeared – the word, along with the notion. Why? Doesn't anyone sin anymore? Doesn't anyone believe in sin?" – Karl Menninger[12]

A Redemption Story

One of the most beloved and remembered literary characters of all time is Ebenezer Scrooge from Charles Dickens' *A Christmas Carol.* Even his name is a study in contrasts. "Scrooge" in our modern vernacular means miserly, stingy, clutch-fisted, and characterizes a person lacking any charity or concern toward others. Interestingly, the "Ebenezer" part of his name means just the opposite. It comes from 1 Samuel 7:12 and represents a stone that was erected by the prophet Samuel after a successful battle against the Philistines. It was a visual reminder of the Lord's power and protection of His people. It was called, "the stone of help." So we see in Ebenezer Scrooge a life nearly ruined by sin but redeemed in the end.

Every year we watch the 1951 Alistair Sim version of the movie and every year we experience the same emotional reaction. We are wowed by Scrooge's incredible disregard and total contempt for suffering humanity. His greed and cynicism betray an underlying depth of sin and depravity which is consuming him. We can almost see a similar weakness in ourselves, an all-consuming selfishness. As the story unfolds we start to feel sorry for him as he faces himself and seeks mercy. Then we are moved by God's goodness in giving him another chance and accepting his repentance. We see in the story how God's grace, love and power can pull any life out of the pit.

Scrooge's story, familiar to many, is actually a picture of redemption. The story begins after the death of his life-long business partner, Bob Marley. Both were shrewd businessmen who lived only to accumulate wealth. Over the years Scrooge became harder and harder as the grip of greed and the idolatry of money consumed him. It squeezed the humanity out of him as the chains grew tighter in his soul. He lost the love of his life, he lost his family, he lost sight of grace. He groused at his only employee, Bob Cratchit, for getting one day a year off with pay. He was a legalist. *"It's not fair that I have to pay you without your doing any work for it."*

Nothing in the story suggested that Ebenezer was a great sinner. He was an upstanding citizen; his work ethic was second to none; no hint of scandal surrounded him. His life showed no evidence of any outward sin unless you consider being stingy a sin. He was totally consumed by his business enterprises and worked at them constantly. The only suggestion of inner sin and struggle was his negative attitude toward helping the impoverished (*"Bah Humbug"*) and his strong approval of the workhouses and debtors' prisons.

The story advances as Marley's ghost appears to Scrooge in his bedchamber. This is a mission of mercy as Marley describes his own massive chains he must drag with him everywhere he goes. He warns Ebenezer of the unseen chains he too was carrying: *"I wear this chain I forged in life. I made it link by link and yard by yard; I girded it of my own free will…it is a ponderous chain."*[13] It was in mercy that Scrooge found his redemption. Over the next three nights, Scrooge would entertain three other ghostly visitors, the Ghosts of Christmas Past, Present and Future. Each revealed Scrooge's life from a different perspective. These exposures opened his eyes to his life, his choices and his destiny should he continue in the same path. He confesses his sin and repents. He is a changed man. He is reborn to a new life as his later actions reveal. Ebenezer becomes the "stone of help" to all, as Dickens ends the story:

> *"Scrooge was better than his word ... and to Tiny Tim, who did not die, he was a second father. He became as good a friend, as good a master, and as good a man as the good old City knew ... and it was always said of him, that he knew how to keep Christmas well."*[4]

It is a heartwarming story that never gets old – as shown by the endless remakes in literature and movies alike.

One of the lessons to us is the revealing of a secret life. Ebenezer's internal sins (choices) of greed and avarice were like an invidious virus, consuming him from the inside out. He did not *look* like a sinner. He probably did not consider himself a sinner and saw himself as a basically "good" person. His was a life that harbored the "acceptable sins," as many of us do. His sins of greed and avarice were not so bad. Maybe he was not even aware that he *was* in sin. Neither was my sin outward. It was, by most accounts, not too bad. Except that, *all* sin carries with it the stigma of sending Christ to the Cross. Not all of us have the hidden sin of greed and avarice that Scrooge harbored. But we all have others sins that flourish in the darkness.

We can look at sin as a continuum ranging from heinous sins on one end to "respectable" sins on the other. From this view my sin, my omission, my unawareness of my sin might be at the "respectable" end of the continuum –a little doubt, some inward rebellion, some unbelief, a bit of envy of others who had an easier time than I had; maybe a bit of lack of trust and of course, some pride. It does not sound very bad, does it? I am in good company, am I not? Many of you see yourselves here, but such minor infractions! It is hardly worth mentioning or thinking about. Why, look at Hitler. I look pretty good next to him. Or, what about a terrorist who goes to his death believing a lie and whose lie takes many innocent lives with him? Think about someone you know – a neighbor or perhaps even someone from the church who you *know* is "living in sin." Their actions are obvious and outward. Some of these people's choices are further up the continuum than our choices. That makes us look like we are closer to God on the holiness scale, doesn't it? Except that is not how sin works.

Over the years, I have read hundreds, maybe thousands, of books. Many of them contained a small section defining sin but never much more than that. As I have labored over this chapter, I have found it challenging to define what sin really is. Because this is not a treatise, a commentary or even a book about theology, I do not plan to try and define it that way. I will tell you what it looks like from my perspective. It is enough for me to know that I was born a sinner, I am still a sinner, but I am on the road to transformation and sanctification, which is wholly a work of God in me.

It was my sin, the nature I was born with and the poor choices I have made that sent Jesus Christ to the Cross. It is enough to put in me a desire to break off habitual sins, things that pull me down and take me off the course of giving my all to Him. It is enough to know that Jesus loved me so much that had I been the only person in eternity to have sinned, He would still have gone to the Cross.

Part of my thinking in naming this book *Stepping Out* was that I saw stepping out of Jesus' footsteps as my sin. I failed to abide by His command to "follow Me" and that failure brought about a series of inner, secret sins which carried unforeseen consequences not outwardly notable. My sin is noteworthy and valuable as a learning tool, not because it is front-page news, but because it *isn't!* These things take us out of fellowship with God and often to lead to painful consequences.

When you read about my words, actions and attitudes in the coming chapters, you might say, "*What's the big deal? This does not seem so bad.*". I think it is important for you to understand what sin is so that you will *see* into your own soul. Some of you have no trouble at all seeing yourself as a sinner – in fact, you have trouble understanding and receiving forgiveness. We will take this up in a later chapter. But others, indeed, most of us, do not even think about it. We are not like Hitler, Idi Amin or other horrible war criminals; we do not outwardly steal, cheat on our spouse or murder anyone, so we do not really think of ourselves as sinners. We know we are if we have been in church or read the Bible, but it just does not seem to matter that much. *"It's such a small thing."* It is like putting a white sheep on a green, pastoral background. They look pretty white – pretty good. But, put them next to a snowy background and you see how dingy and dirty they really are! Next to Hitler, most of us admittedly look pretty good. However, put us next to the beauty and perfection of Jesus Christ and we see who we really are.

In the next chapter, we will look at defining the binding chains. *What is sin? I thought it was finished when I became a believer. What's the big deal anyway – such small sins. How can they matter?*

Chapter 4. Unlocking the Binding Chains

"Therefore this is what the Sovereign Lord says: 'I am against your magic charms with which you ensnare people like birds and I will tear them from your arms; I will set free the people that you ensnare like birds. I will tear off your veils and save my people from your hands, and they will no longer fall prey to your power. Then you will know that I am the Lord.'" -- Ezekiel 13:20-21 (NIV)

"You sin because you are a sinner. We are born warped. Sin must be removed." – Pastor Mike Reed, Calvary Chapel Oceanside15

A Picture of a Soul Gone Bad

I have always been mesmerized by the story by Oscar Wilde, *The Picture of Dorian Gray*. As both a book and the movie, it is a chilling snapshot of what sin in the soul can look like. I prefer the 1945 movie but there are more recent ones available also. The story begins in a London studio where an artist (Basil) is putting the finishing touches on his latest portrait. It is of a young and extremely handsome young man named Dorian Gray. One of his visitors, Lord Henry, a decadent n'er do well who lives only for pleasure, beauty and all that life offers in the dark recesses of London's underworld, finds out who the young man is and proceeds to influence him to his way of thinking.

Lord Henry tells Dorian that he must guard his youth and beauty while he still has them, as it will fade. Dorian, terrified of losing his youth, wishes he could trade his soul to stay as young as he looks in the portrait. Be careful what you wish for! When Dorian falls in love with a young, unspoiled actress Sybil, who must take to the stage to survive, they decide to marry. However, with Lord Henry's evil hissing and Dorian's own nature, Dorian ends up with a disgust of her and he breaks off the wedding. Dorian goes home to inspect the portrait only to see lines of cruelty forming about the mouth. He is frightened and vows to do better. Before he could return to Sybil, she commits suicide and Dorian's path is set.

He received a book from Lord Henry, his "mentor" in the dark side of life and the treacherous book of evil becomes Dorian's bible. He enters into a life of murder, drugs and dark sin. Through the years Dorian continues to look young and fresh but he is hiding a secret. The portrait, now hidden in the attic, shows signs of the life he is living as it takes on a hideous portrayal of evil incarnate. When Basil, the original artist asks to see the portrait, he is horrified and begs Dorian to seek forgiveness, repent of his sin and revoke the wish he made so many years ago. Instead, Dorian kills Basil and hides the body.

Warning: Spoiler Alert

Dorian never does repent and the story ends with his taking the same knife he used to kill Basil to the painting. Not long after, his servants find an old, unrecognizable, horribly deformed, shriveled man lying dead on the floor of the attic. Standing next to him was a slashed but stunning picture of a beautiful young man.

Defining Sin – Or Not

Sin is not easy to define in today's culture. I feel like Justice Stewart Potter of the U.S. Supreme Court as he tried to define "obscenity" in a 1964 case. He stated he was not sure how to define it, but *"I know it when I see it."* The evil resident within us is so deceptive and destructive it is almost impossible to define all of its avenues.

I originally wrote this chapter by defining the Old Testament and New Testament words for sin, but it was too preachy, a bit esoteric and not easily applicable. To boil down the definitions, I came up with this:

"Whereas our sin nature is something we are born with, our sins are made up of things that we do, something we say to ourselves, others or God, or an attitude that arises in the heart that misses God's standard. The New Testament word **harmartia** *literally means to 'miss the mark.'"*

Lawrence O. Richards says:

"Sin is not only missing God's mark; it is an inner reality, a warp in human nature and a malignant power that holds each individual in an unbreakable grip."[16]

All of us miss the mark. Romans 3:23 says, *"For all have sinned and fallen short of the glory of God."* Even Ecclesiastes has a word on the subject. In 7:20 it says, *"Indeed, there is not a righteous man on earth who continually does good and who never sins."*

The Problem with Dos and Don'ts

The real problem with defining sin is its many forms. There are numerous sin lists in the Bible. For example, see Matthew 15, Romans 1 and Mark 6. The lists in themselves do not capture the whole concept of sin. And most of us would select sins from these lists that we would try to avoid. Growing in understanding, we would keep adding new sins to the avoid list in an effort to please God. This growing legalism would weigh us down to the point where we would want to give up.

As a very young Christian I combed the Bible looking for "how to live", making lists of dos and don'ts, not realizing that almost every story contained a lesson in sin or forgiveness. I did fairly well on the outward sins I saw because of my fear of consequences, but I could not conquer the inward sins – doubt, pride, anger, unbelief, rebellion (though not outward), greed, envy and others and, frankly, at times I could not see those things in myself.

The Deeper Problem

Behind our sins, there is a deeper root of rebellion within us, which the Bible calls "sin" (singular), which is our inherited sin nature. (Romans 5:12) Because of this sin nature within us, we choose to go our own way (i.e., putting other things in the place of God), rebel in some way, or fail to trust in Him totally and solely. Even as believers we do not take Him at His Word; we do not obey what He has told us in His Word; we think we know better or we fail to understand His call to follow and do not see that our disobedience to His Word is part of the sin that takes us out. Our own theology sounds good to us, but may in truth disagree with His Word. I have experienced that myself, even after having studied the Bible for many years.

We tend to try and deal with our sins in our own strength, if we try at all. We may be surprised by **the depth of our own capacity to do evil.** We often call on our will to help us. But our will cannot help because *sin* is our nature.

The Divine Solution

We must have a solution that takes care of that problem. It would involve an inner transformation so that we can be freed from the dominion of evil or the nature (*sin*) we were born into: an opportunity to resist and say no. Enter Jesus Christ and His *salvation.* He came to set the captives free and His death and resurrection made possible a way to free the soul from the nature of sin. He came to free, forgive and make whole. Thus, now we have another piece to the concept of *salvation,* which we discussed in Chapter Two.

Because God is holy, a price must be paid for committing any sin. So, in essence, either I have to pay or someone else who is qualified has to pay in my place. Only one Person in the history of the world is qualified to take your sin and mine on Himself: Jesus Christ. The way I put it is, *"Either I pay or He pays."* If I pay, I live an eternity without His Presence because I cannot pay the price. If He pays, my future is set.

In the New Testament we learn the remedy for our sin nature (the blood shed by Christ on the Cross), where our sins originate (in the heart/soul) and learn for the first time of the power resident in us to say "no." It is in the process of sanctification, of becoming like Christ, where we can turn away from habitual sin as we walk humbly with Him. Drawing nearer to Him on the journey, seeking Him with our whole heart and surrendering all are pieces along the way to help us in this venture.

A Summary of Sin in the Believer

Let's review these concepts to help ground us further. Look up the Scripture and jot down some notes in your journal about your findings.

- Sin is a matter of the heart (Matthew 15:16-20).
- Some sin is instinctively known to us (Romans 1:18-32).
- Sins are committed through words, attitudes or actions.
- We are born with a sin nature and we all sin (Romans 3:23 and 5:12).
- Through Jesus and His death on the Cross, we receive forgiveness once and for all (1 Peter 2:24).
- Through Jesus we have the possibility of a newly generated life from the inside out (2 Corinthians 5:21).
- Through Jesus, we receive the capacity NOT to sin (our new nature). We can choose (Romans 7:6).
- By surrender to God and reliance on the Holy Spirit, the sin nature in each of us can be "dampened." We can choose "no" (Romans 8:1-3).
- We still need to ask forgiveness for our sins, which restores fellowship with Him (John 16:8).
- The power and reality of His living in us gives us a major motivation not to continue in habitual sin (1 John 3:7-9).

How is Sin Revealed in Our Lives?

We learn from John 16:8 that the Holy Spirit is the One who convicts the world (including believers) of sin. He is not only the Comforter, Counselor and Guide, He is the One who exposes our sin and lets us know somehow that we are out of fellowship with God. *How* He convicts is as varied as the people He created.

In Scrooge's life, his sin was revealed through dreams of heavenly visitors coming to reveal to heal. In my life, my sin was revealed through my daily journal writings. By jotting down the activities of the day, the things I was reading and learning in Scripture and other places and writing about my thoughts, feelings and struggles, I was able to *see*. Two years after writing about the struggles, I was looking through the recent journal entries for some stories to use at a retreat I was scheduled to speak at. It was then that I saw the answer to the silence and dryness I had been experiencing in my spiritual life. The Holy Spirit revealed my sin in the words of my own writing!

But you might not keep a journal. There are other ways He reveals. Some of you have children who mirror your actions or remind you when you step out; others hear things in sermons or podcasts or books that pierce your heart; still others have a painful unveiling, not unlike what David experienced after his sin with Bathsheba. The best way to learn about sin is through your time in the Word. It reveals sin, such as in the terrible twelve Jesus speaks of in Matthew 15 and Mark 7:20-23. Paul speaks often of sin as he comes to grip with it in his own life. (See Romans 1:28-31) There is no lack of knowledge of sin in the writers of the Bible. Their lives, like ours, tell the tale. And the Spirit will reveal in ways we can hear if we but listen.

Beware of the Enemy's Deceptive Techniques

But be careful here. Beware of the accuser who comes to bury you with his accusations, pile your sins on you until you are smothered, hopeless and unable to see through. That is NOT how the Holy Spirit reveals. Jesus spoke of His Spirit as One who is,

"... sent by the Father to teach you and remind you of Jesus' words to us; He is the One who guides us into all truth and will speak to you only what He hears; He will bring glory to Jesus even in His revealing of truth." -- John 14:26, 16:13, 14

That is not the way the enemy comes. As we will see in later chapters, God's Spirit will always give warnings and clues when we take a wrong path. If those are not enough to deter us, more warnings and clues might come. But when God's Spirit convicts us of missing the mark by calling us to acknowledge our wrong words, attitudes or actions, He gives us the avenue of repenting, being cleansed and receiving forgiveness. At the same time He comforts, promising restoration and reassurance of His love. We learn in Psalm 51:6-7,

"Surely you (God) desire truth in the inner parts; you teach me wisdom in the inmost place. Cleanse me with hyssop, and I will be clean; wash me and I will be whiter than snow." (NIV)

He will never burden us with all of our sins at once, but gently reveals to heal, selecting those areas in our soul that most need attention now. He reveals a piece at a time, not to overwhelm us, but to guide us into truth. This guidance may require that He use increasingly stronger warnings and methods to get our attention, sometimes allowing consequences for our choices. But it is always done only in love. Hebrews 12:7-13 explains it.

So many times we do not see our sin and do not see the need to repent and be cleansed. Thus when things in the soul dry up we wonder why we are not living in joy and abundance, which should be a gentle warning right there. Alternatively, if we do see, we beat ourselves up, feeling like the worst of the worst who couldn't possibly be forgiven again. So we often have trouble receiving His assurance of love and forgiveness. But it is when we surrender that He reveals to heal. In Psalm 139:1 and 7, we can groan with David as he says,

"O Lord, you have searched me and you know me...you perceive my thoughts from afar...Where can I go from your Spirit, where can I flee from Your presence?"

It is always His love, always His choice to call us back to Him. He is unrelenting in His love and care for us. He will never stop pursuing us to bring us back into fellowship when we fall. In His love He will "do what it takes" to bring us back. David understood this truth. We will look at this Biblical example in the next chapter.

Chapter 5. A Painful Betrayal – A Biblical Example

"If we are faithless, he remains faithful, for he cannot deny himself." – 2 Timothy 2:13

"As long as your sin breaks your heart, as long as your disobedience makes you lie awake at night and wet your pillow in tears, there is hope for you." -- Clovis G. Chappell

Sin's Wide Compass

As I have explained, sin embraces our actions, words and attitudes that miss God's standard. While this book mostly deals with the inner words and attitudes of the soul, our outward actions play a part as well. These are the sins that all can see for they are the most familiar to us. Our own poor choices and others' sinful actions, which affect us, can also impact our soul. As we will see in this chapter, sin has a ripple effect. It touches not only us individually, but our family, our future, our church, our community and others in our world.

One of the most familiar characters in the Bible is David. When we were young, we learned of his victory against Goliath; as we grew older, we learned of his sin with Bathsheba. Yet he was a called a "friend of God." God loved him despite his somewhat tragic life. There is hope for us all!

The familiar story of David and Bathsheba created not just a ripple effect but a tsunami. It impacted David's health, his family, Bathsheba's family and her household. Even the nation over which David ruled was not immune to the impact of his sin. Such is the nature of stepping out! God does not discipline us because He is a mean God, but because He better than anyone understands the pain and trauma sin can generate. Romans 8 tells us that even nature groans under the weight of our sin (Romans 8:19-21).

When David should have been at war with his men, he was found instead languishing on his rooftop. In 2 Samuel 12, after David's sin with Bathsheba, the prophet Nathan told David a story about a man who stole another man's ewe lamb. David became incensed and angry when he heard the story. Then Nathan pointed his bony finger at David and said, *"You are the man!"* When David saw himself in the story, he was broken. He saw. He recognized that his sin was not against any person, but that, *"I have sinned against God alone"* (12:13). Psalm 51 is the psalm connected with this story and is one of the most amazing and clearest passages in the Bible on repentance. We will take this up in Part Two of the book when we speak on repentance as a war strategy.

Stop here and read 2 Samuel 12. Make a note of consequences from David's life of what his rebellion cost him and those around him. To get you started, consider these consequences:

- He missed out on what God had in store for him: *"I would have given you so much more"* (2 Samuel 12:8).
- He would have a consequence in that his family in the future would: *"live by the sword because of what you have done"* (2 Samuel 12:10).
- His own household would rebel (2 Samuel 12:11).
- His dirty secret was exposed to all. A man lauded and admired by all was now being whispered about during the dinner hour and by gossiping women at the well (2 Samuel 12:12).
- His sin was taken away by God but the consequences were not (2 Samuel 12:13).
- He himself would not lose his life, but his son would (2 Samuel 12:14).

- Finally, his sin gave his enemies a place from which to blaspheme God (2 Samuel 12:14).

What else do you see? David is an example for us to *not* follow his ways and fall into sin. And yet 2 Samuel 12:24 says, *"Now the Lord loved him…"* God does not always give us a consequence for our actions; sometimes He dispenses grace instead. But whether it is grace or consequence, it is always done in love.

Consequences of Disobedience

There is an interesting story I would like you to stop and read in 2 Samuel 24:10-14. This event occurred after the Bathsheba affair. David recognized his actions in taking a census of the fighting men as a sin. Elsewhere we learn that at one point Satan incited David to take a census (1 Chronicles 21:1). And in the Samuel passage, verse 1, it says that God incited David to take the census. God did not tempt David or cause him to sin, but He brought out that which was in David already. Whatever is not of faith is sin and David relied, not on his faith in God, but in the numbers of the troops he had amassed.

It was the enemy tempting him to find security in numbers, not in God to which David gave in. On the other hand, it was the sin of David's pride that God was highlighting and showing him. Doing a census in and of itself was not a sin; just as seeing Bathsheba on the roof was not sin. It was the giving into temptation that was.

In our own lives, we can replace "census" with anything God says not to do. The Bible is full of things to avoid – using phrases like "shall not" or "must not". God gives us these directives, not because He is a cosmic killjoy, but because He has a high standard. His love for us motivates Him to give us these commands. "Whatever is not of faith is sin" (Romans 14:23). It is a failure and a sin **not** to trust God in everything. We should learn this principle well.

There is so much to this census story that I would love to share with you, but what I think is important for you to see is how David handled his sin once he became aware of it. He saw his wrongdoing without being confronted this time and he immediately went into repentance and confession. When the prophet of the day, Gad, came to him the following morning, David was given the choice of three consequences: seven years of famine; three months of pursuit by his enemies; or three days of pestilence in the land. The prophet said in verse 13, *"Now consider and see what answer I shall return to Him who sent me."* David was quick to answer and his answer expresses his understanding of the depth of God's love for him: *"I am in great distress. Let us now fall into the hand of the Lord for His mercies are great, but do not let me fall into the hand of man"* (verse 14). David understood it was far better to fall into the hands of a loving, merciful God than into any earthly enemy. Oh, that we could know the depths of His love for us even when we sin.

Part of the journey of walking closer with Jesus and living a more abundant life involves allowing Him to lead us to a place of seeing our sin and pressing in to Him for forgiveness, cleansing and restoration. Not just the "big" sins, the outward sins that everyone sees, but the inner sins – the ones we tolerate; the ones we hide, even from ourselves. I am convinced that as you continue reading this book and read about my journey and the inward sin I was harboring, you will be able to look at your own life with a sense of clarity and purpose. Freedom is on the way!

Chapter 6. An Orphan's Story

"I will not leave you as orphans; I will come to you." – John 14:18 (Jesus speaking)

"We were all born with an orphan heart…our quest is to enter into the embrace of the unconditional love of Father God and receive a heart of sonship that will displace our orphan heart." – Jack Frost[17]

Recognizing Toxic Words

In the movie *Lord of the Rings: The Two Towers*, based on the novel by J.R.R. Tolkien, there is a scene between Grima Wormtongue and Eowyn the niece of King Theoden. Grima Wormtongue was the malevolent counselor to the king who kept him in a stupor of oppression and bondage. When Eowyn's brother died, the slimy snake writhes into her boudoir to work his poison on her:

> **Grima Wormtongue to Eowyn**: *His passing must be hard to accept now that your brother has deserted you.* **Eowyn**: *Leave me alone, you snake!*

> **Wormtongue**: *Oh, but **you are alone**. Who knows what you have spoken to the darkness, alone, in the bitter watches of the night, when all your life seems to shrink, the walls of your bower closing in about you, a hutch to trammel some wild thing in? So fair, yet so cold like a morning of pale Spring still clinging to Winter's chill.* **Eowyn**: *Your words are poison!*

Eowyn might have felt alone but she knew enough to recognize the toxic words for the lies they contained. It is a tool we also must incorporate into our arsenal. Movies, when carefully selected, watched with intentionality and a desire to see, can teach us principles for living life in the Spirit. Our family watches *The Hobbit*

Trilogy and *The Lord of the Rings Trilogy* every year over the Christmas holidays. I am always amazed by how closely their journey mirrors ours.

A Parable to Consider

I was recently invited to attend an evening with a group of women who were gathering in groups to study my first book, *The Call to Follow Jesus: Studies in the Gospel of Mark.* I asked the group, who were in various stages of the study, to share what they were learning about following Jesus. Tracy, one of the leaders, had a marvelous story to tell. With her permission, I report it here.

She had just returned from a safari in Africa and shared her experience. Ready for adventure, the group entered the jeep with the guide. When they got to the first sighting area, the guide told everyone to step out of the jeep and line up behind him. After looking around, Tracy felt it would be safer to stay in the jeep rather than join the group. The leader insisted she stay with the group. *"You're much safer with us. If you refuse to get out of the jeep, you might become prey for one of the more aggressive animals."* That was all Tracy needed to motivate her and she immediately scrambled out and got in line. The next thing the guide told the group was that they needed to follow him precisely and carefully. *"Do exactly what I do. If I crouch, you crouch; if I jump, you jump, if I yell, you yell."* The reason, he explained, was that there was safety in numbers and, if everyone did the same thing, they would intimidate the animals by the largeness of the group. Believing them to be one giant predator, they would be less likely to attack. He very soberly informed them that if they wandered off on their own or got out of line, he was not responsible for what happened. Not one person in that group missed a beat in following that leader! And everyone made it back without a scratch.

I love this story because it so perfectly describes following in Jesus' footsteps, which is the call of every believer. Though each of us has a different path prepared for us, as we learn to follow Him, do exactly what He does and go where He leads, we will see things we never thought to see. But as we have all clearly experienced in life, there is the up-side (being *in* His footsteps), and there is the down-side (stepping *out* of His footsteps). We have a vile enemy who does not want us to succeed. As Donna Partow[18] says, *"God loves you and has a wonderful plan for your life. Satan hates you and has a horrible plan for your life."*

Tracy's little parable really is descriptive of the believer's walk. Having wandered away and stepped out of His footsteps myself, I have become aware of just how vicious the attack of the enemy can be. I was already unknowingly harboring an orphan spirit in my soul, and stepping out isolated me even more, cutting me off from family, friends, my own internal alarms, God's warnings and most importantly, God's protection.

The Orphan Spirit

In 2015, I was sitting in a class at a writer's conference at Mount Hermon, California. It was a class, not about writing, but about the soul of a writer. I didn't know what I was getting into. It was one of the things God used to change the direction of my life. In the class, the facilitator, Allen Arnold of *Ransomed Heart Ministries* talked about the concept of writing *with God* not just for Him. I understood that concept, but when he began to delve into soul stuff, I was familiar with what he was speaking of, but not on a heart level. I was unprepared for the visceral reaction I had to some of his comments. He began to speak about deserts and places of isolation. He asked questions like,

> *"Do you ever feel alone; no one is there for you; no one is with you in this journey; if you don't do it, it won't get done; always have a back-up plan because it's all up to you?"*

In my head I'm answering yes to every question, thinking, *"Doesn't everyone feel this way?"* This way of thinking had been with me so long I didn't know any other way to think. I had written about these very things in my journal a couple of years before without any awareness of the devastation those words would bring.

Then Allen said this: *"If any of these questions describe you, you have an orphan spirit."* I had never heard that phrase before but the reaction was like being punched in the stomach. There I sat in the middle of the crowded room, doubled over, sobbing, as usual without a tissue. Concerned people near me started sending tissues down the row. It was so embarrassing. I felt naked, like being the star of a bad dream. But in that moment God spoke to me. He said, *"That's you and I am going to heal you of this orphan spirit."*

At that very moment, I recognized it. In a flash, I saw throughout my whole life these feelings had been there. It had been part of my journey for so long and I was completely unaware of it. I knew that God was with me, but I was often disappointed to feel I was somehow going it alone on the journey. It is what I call a *heart-head disconnect*. I knew in my head I wasn't alone, but my heart and soul couldn't experience it. I prayed for help, but for the most part thought it was still up to me. I always had a back-up plan in case things went awry (that, by the way, might be called "controlling"). It sometimes seemed to me that God sat me down in the middle of the desert and said, *"Okay. Go. Do my Will."* It was all up to me! No! No! No! Lies, all lies! I was easy prey for the enemy. I was the best kind of prisoner – the clueless kind because I didn't *know!*

I wasn't an orphan physically. I had a great family and a pretty good life growing up. Where did it come from? Having been healed from that, I can now look back and see some of its beginnings. Both of my grandmothers were orphans, one getting on a ship in Glasgow, Scotland at age sixteen and coming to Ellis Island to find a cousin she had never met. The other, having lost her own mother at age three, was placed in an orphanage while her other three siblings were parceled out to other relatives so their father could marry a woman who didn't want someone else's children. My grandmother somehow managed to keep up with her siblings and as the years passed, grew close to them, held together with a glue only God could provide.

Being the oldest of four siblings, the orphan spirit that my grandmothers experienced physically fell on me spiritually. There was no other explanation for me to feel the way I was feeling or experiencing the pain of isolation and feelings of abandonment I was secretly carrying. I often felt no one liked me or wanted me around, even though I could count hundreds of friends and acquaintances who seemed to have no problem with me.

Throughout my life I have had lots of friends – good friends, lifelong friends who have never abandoned me; I have an amazing husband who loves me, even when I'm at my worst! My parents didn't experience it. My sisters didn't experience it, though I believe my brother may have. Where did it come from? How did this spirit attach to me? When God exposed it at the conference, I had immediate understanding.

How It Happens

This would be a good place to stop and consider the issue of how demons intersect with Christians. I am sure this has already been simmering in your mind. Many churches do not deal with this issue head-on and many, perhaps even the one you are attending, might disagree with what I have experienced in my life in recent years. Practically all mainline churches teach that demons cannot *possess* true believers. This is consistent with Biblical teaching. But this is where a diversion occurs. While many believers follow up this teaching by saying that demons therefore have no dealings at all with Christians, I have found that not to be the case in my own life.

A man I respect very much, Dr. Charles Kraft, explains that, while believers cannot be possessed by demons, demons can *attach* to the garbage (what I call baggage) in a believer's soul. When a believer comes to Christ, his or her spirit is indwelled by God's Spirit and no demonic activity can take place there. But our soul, as we have already discussed, contains baggage that remains. Consider emotional and spiritual issues such as traumas from our childhood, word-curses put on us by our own talk or others', wounds, and unconfessed sins committed since coming to Christ. It might even include generational baggage such as my grandmothers experienced. Dr. Kraft calls these things "garbage". He explains that the rats (demons) attach to these things in our soul and feeds on them. Once we get rid of the garbage, the rats will leave! (This simple answer colorfully depicts the freedom in the soul that we are exploring in this book.) His book[19] contains more information, if you want to explore this area more.

Look at some of these Biblical references for further study:

- 2 Timothy 1:7: "For God did not give us a **spirit of fear** but a spirit of power, of love and self-discipline."
- 1 John 4:6: "This is how we recognize the Spirit of truth and the **spirit of falsehood…**"
- Matthew 12:43: "When an **evil spirit** comes out of a man…"
- Isaiah 61:1 and 3: "…the Lord has anointed me [Jesus] to bestow on them [His children] …a garment of praise instead of a **spirit of despair…**"
- Hosea 5:4 (speaking of His people): "A **spirit of prostitution** is in their heart; they do not acknowledge the Lord."

This is only a sample. Please be sure to read the verses in context and ask God's Spirit to check yours and speak to the truthfulness of the Scripture verses.

This is part of my story. I was unable to get enough freedom to write the books I was being called to write without understanding this area.

I have mentioned several times in this book that when we experience wounds, pain, trauma or betrayal, either self-inflicted or inflicted by others, the enemy gets a toehold in to our lives. He uses the various painful events throughout our life to attach to and create pain and disorder. If they are not dealt with through Christ, the enemy gains more territory.

When we come to Christ, although we are completely forgiven, the hurts we experienced throughout life come with us and those areas also need salvation. Recall our definition of salvation, which includes healing, rescue, deliverance, wholeness. If those painful areas are not addressed, the toehold can become a foothold, a stronghold or a stranglehold on us keeping us from experiencing all that God designed us for.

Strongholds are formed by thought patterns that develop when we allow the enemy to build a fortress around a particular thought, event or area in our life. And they must be toppled in order to experience freedom. In the next chapter, we will discuss this and more as we look at the connection between spiritual attachments and the past generations of our family.

Chapter 7. Generational Bondage and Blessing

"Behold, all souls are Mine; the soul of the father as well as the soul of the son is Mine. The soul who sins will die. But if a man is righteous and practices justice and righteousness,... if he walks in My statutes and My ordinances so as to deal faithfully -- he is righteous and will surely live," declares the Lord GOD."
-- Ezekiel 18:4, 5, 9

"The way we live is serious. What we do affects our children and our grandchildren...When we walk in righteousness, the next generation and the next generation are going to be blessed because of us." -- Marilyn Hickey[20]

Biblical Precedent

There is precedent in the Bible for both generational bondage and generational blessing. You may have heard the phrase, *"the sins of the fathers are visited on the children to the third and fourth generations."* This comes from Exodus 20:4-6, the second of the Ten Commandments, which contains a warning and a promise:

"You shall not make for yourself an idol, or any likeness of what is in heaven above or on the earth beneath or in the water under the earth. You shall not worship them or serve them; for I, the Lord your God, am a jealous God, visiting the iniquity of the fathers on the children, on the third and the fourth generations of those who hate Me, but showing loving-kindness to thousands, to those who love Me and keep My commandments."

Let me say beforehand that not all pastors and scholars agree upon the issue of generational bondage. Some definitively say there is no doctrine of generational bondage, and the reasons they give are good. Others say the Bible clearly teaches the doctrine. This is a subject you

47

will need to take to prayer in your own life. I am only telling you my story.

What most pastors *do* agree on is that what you do will impact generations to come. If you are godly and raise your children in that manner, their future will be positively impacted in some way (Exodus 20:6). On the other hand, if you live loosely and in disobedience, without regard for God and steep yourself in worshiping any person, thing, or object other than God, that will negatively impact future generations (Exodus 20:5). You have the power to influence future generations for good or evil by your actions. Adam's faulty words, actions and attitudes (sin) in the garden influenced mankind through every generation and flows from his sin to all of us. We did nothing to inherit the curse. (Romans 5:12 and 1 Corinthians 15:22).

Our sins, our choices right now matter. They impact generations to come both inside of our families and outside. We do not live unto ourselves alone. Someone in the future will be impacted by the good or bad choices I make now. What we do in secret will impact our future, our children's future, and maybe even our grandchildren's future. My grandmothers' orphan journeys were impacted by their family choices and their life circumstances. They did not blame their families nor do I.

What the verses do not mean is that parents, grandparents and others in our bloodline can be blamed for what we are going through now. You cannot just abrogate responsibility. That is not Biblical. Do not blame your parents for the situation you currently find yourself in. Go to God to give forgiveness and find it. Be cleansed, and break off the sin by breaking the agreement you or your ancestors might have had with the enemy. Then move on. We will discuss this more in Chapter 16.

I am seeking deeper relationship with God because I love Him and hunger for more of His presence in my life. There is an additional blessing in Psalm 112:1-2 that says,

"How blessed is the man who fears the Lord, who greatly delights in His commandments. His descendants will be mighty on earth; the generation of the upright will be blessed. Wealth and riches are in his house. And his righteousness endures forever."

I am seeking Him now, not for what He can do for my family, and me but for Himself alone. Because of that, I believe my son's life will be blessed; his children will be blessed and so it follows through the generations. It is the "exceedingly, abundantly beyond" (Ephesians 3:20) part of God's nature to give and give and give.

Overcoming in this area has to do with relinquishing attachments and surrendering all to Him. Rabbi K.A. Schnieder, a Messianic Rabbi says,

"Jesus wanted His followers to understand that if they did not relinquish every attachment, even those primary generational relationships, to become bonded to Him, they would continue to struggle in some areas of their lives." [21]

The Hebrew word for "visit" is *paqadh*, which also means to *"visit upon, review, deposit."* These verses do not necessarily mean that we will be punished (though that is one meaning for *paqadh*) for the sins of our ancestors. Remember, I said there was a warning and a promise in these verses? (Exodus 20:4-6) The warning may mean that the sins of our ancestors will be revisited on us and we will suffer from the consequences of their sin if the curse is not broken. But the promise is that God in His mercy chooses to revisit each person for their own life and review each person's life independently.

Beloved, what this is saying is that, if the iniquity of past generations persists, He will *visit again and again*, giving opportunity to know Him, to be changed by Him, to be freed by Him. That is what I believe I experienced. I did not know why I was so miserable, subject to depression, darkness and feelings of abandonment. The truth is, my grandmothers were not wanted. They were orphans and that spirit settled on them because of *their* parents' pain and subsequent actions. It followed through the generations and somehow found its way into my life. Ezekiel 18:4 and 9 say this:

> *"Behold, ALL souls are Mine, the soul of the father as well as the soul of a son is Mine. The soul who sins will die. But if a man is righteous, and practices justice and righteousness...he is righteous and will live."*

There is hope for your future and your children's. You do not need to stay in bondage to actions perpetrated by your former ancestors and the bondage you are under need not follow to your children and grandchildren. You can be the generation that breaks things off from future generations.

If you are one of the many godly parents or grandparents who have raised your children in faith and are not seeing the fruit in their lives, do not give up praying. His answers come in different ways and the power of your prayers is stronger than you know or see. The enemy would like you to give up in despair, but do not give up praying. I have a brother on the streets. I have not ceased praying for him since he was twelve. I have seen him come to Christ with what I believe is a genuine repentant spirit, but he still lives on the streets. I cannot understand why the power of God has not freed him, but I also know I do not have the whole picture. I choose to continue in faith to pray and expect God to heal him or call him home. God sees where we do not. Beloved, when you can't trace His hand, trust His heart in this journey. For me, to understand the orphan spirit, there was no other explanation.

I would also say to you to work on your own soul now. Even as you continue in prayer for your wayward child, shore up your own soul, get freedom from the things that take you down, learn to use the weapons of war talked about in this book. Pray and ask God to reveal generational bondage in your bloodline and in your spouse's. Learn to worship and praise Him, standing firm against the enemy in your own life. This will infuse strength to pray and act to which the enemy will have to pay attention to and bow. Do not give up.

Family Dispositions

The Bible speaks of curses and bondage in the land. It also teaches about curses and bondage affecting families over generations. We can see inherited problems in our own families, showing up as health issues of the body, mind or emotions. While the Bible is very clear that each of us answers for our own sin, families have predispositions or weaknesses to various sin categories that can impact future generations.

Scientists both secular and Christian are saying much the same thing in the study of a relatively new field of science called epigenetics:

> *"Epigenetics suggests that a person's choices and experience have biological effects that can be passed to the next generation, even to future generations."*[22]

The studies basically reveal that, while we inherit certain traits from our parents and ancestors, both the good and bad, the path can be broken or changed so that we are not prisoners of our family's past.

If you have ever filled out an insurance form or a health form, you have probably been asked whether someone in your family has had diabetes, heart disease or cancer. One explanation is that these diseases are hereditary or can impact future generations. Other curses include divorce, alcoholism, poverty, pornography, racism, bitterness, negative thinking, verbal or physical abuse.

However, these things are not always generational. Sometimes *we* are the generation that starts the curses. Beth Moore says:

> *"A crucial reason exists for facing our generational strongholds head on: Unless we purposely seek them, they can remain almost unrecognizable, but they will not remain benign. Family ruins continue to be seedbeds for all sorts of destructions in our lives. We tend to think of generational hand-me-down baggage*

as part of who we are rather than how we're bound. In many cases we grew up with these chains, so they feel completely natural. We're apt to consider them part of our personalities rather than a yoke squeezing abundant life out of us."[23]

I agree with Beth. My feelings about myself, my bondage, and my orphanhood felt like it was just who I was. Breaking the bondage wherever it is found is part of Jesus' job description. It is Who He is. It is why He came (Isaiah 61:1-4). There is hope, hope, hope from the God of all hope who will, *"fill you with all joy and peace as you trust in him so that you may overflow with hope by the power of the Holy Spirit"* (Romans 15:13). We will explore breaking bondage and curses further in Chapter 16.

Let's sum up God's attitude toward us in this paraphrase from Exodus 20:2-6:

"I am your God. I bought you with a price. I paid for your freedom by the blood on the doorpost. Do not bow to idols. Do not worship any image, thing, person or object except Me. I am jealous for you because you are being robbed and deceived. I want you to be blessed and experience all that I have for you. I am your Father. I am Abba – daddy. I want to show mercy to you and I will visit you over and over again, never getting tired of pursuing relationship with you – no matter who you are, what you have done, what your parents, grandparents or great, great grandparents have done. You do not need to blame anyone else. I can redeem any sin in your life, whether it had its beginnings in your distant past or your present life. You are Mine. I love you."

In the next chapter, we will look at a prophet's life, one who considered himself an orphan.

Chapter 8. Life of a Biblical Orphan

"Never will I leave you; never will I forsake you." – Hebrews 13:5b (NIV)

"I am the only one left, and now they are trying to kill me, too." – (Elijah) 1 Kings 19:10b

Orphans Unaware

There is Biblical precedence for orphans unaware. The greatest prophet who ever lived (besides Jesus), was Elijah. He had his moments of despair and unbelief just like the rest of us. But he also wrongly believed himself to be an orphan. Let's look together at 1 Kings 18-19. I'd like you to read it over in your Bible. Then, let's talk.

In context, Elijah was a prophet of God who lived during one of the most difficult and evil times in Israel's history. The infamous couple Ahab and Jezebel were on the throne, but in reality, Jezebel herself ruled the land with an iron fist. Idolatry was everywhere. There were over four hundred and fifty prophets of Baal and four hundred prophets of Asherah sitting at Jezebel's table, spreading their poison among God's people. The phrase *"sitting at the King's table"* was a position of power and authority.

You can understand from this that wickedness had overtaken Israel in a big way. And all the while, Jezebel was hunting down and killing God's chosen prophets. God sent Elijah alone to face her prophets in battle on Mount Carmel. There are no adequate words to explain just how bad things really were in Israel. Jezebel may have been the most treacherous, vile woman who ever lived. In fact, many believers today think her spirit lives on and still impacts nations, churches and individuals. Indeed, in Revelation 2:20, Jesus certainly believed her spirit is alive and active. He says to the church at Thyatira,

> *"But I have this against you, that you tolerate the woman Jezebel, who calls herself a prophetess, and she teaches and leads My bond-servants astray so that they commit acts of immorality and eat things sacrificed to idols."*

Elijah was terrified of her, and rightly so. After Elijah, with God's help, destroyed the prophets of Baal and Asherah on Mount Carmel, 1 Kings 18:46 says that, *"The power of the Lord came upon Elijah and, tucking his cloak into his belt, he ran ahead of Ahab all the way to Jezreel."* (NIV) That is mighty fast running as Ahab was in his chariot! Ahab was trying to get to Jezebel to tell her what happened. As you read in 1 Kings 19:1-2, when she found out, she was furious. The NIV Study Bible[24] says that the words here are words of cursing. *"May the gods deal with me, ever so severely, if by this time tomorrow I do not make your life like that of one of them [the dead prophets]."* (NIV) Jezebel put a curse on Elijah seeking his death.

In 1 Samuel 3:17 the prophet Eli asked Samuel to tell him what God was saying to him and he used a similar formula, *"May God deal with you, be it ever so severely, if you hide from me anything he told you."*

The Power of a Word Curse

> *A curse is the opposite of a blessing. A curse is described in part as, "People of the ancient world considered that curses were major tools to be used to gain power over their enemies." Old Testament nations considered curses as, "magical incantations that harnessed supernatural power to harm enemies." From the Biblical perspective (as in the Samuel passage noted in the text), "A curse may be uttered as a solemn oath or warning of what God will do if His covenant is violated. A curse may also be a judgment itself, spoken of after it has been imposed. Such a curse binds and limits its object. It brings diminished circumstances that stand in contrast to the blessing God yearns*

to provide." – culled from the Expository Dictionary of Bible Words.[25]

Word curses are powerful and Elijah understood their power. We learn in 1 Kings 19:3 that he was so frightened of the words that he, "*arose and ran for his life*" leaving all, including his servant, behind. The power of this woman's words was so forceful that Scripture records in 19:4, that Elijah, "*requested for himself that he might die.*" He felt totally alone even after God sent His angels to care for him. After eating, Elijah got up and went to Mount Horeb, at the other end of the kingdom, and hid in a cave.

Horeb is called *the mountain of God* (1 Kings 19:18). It is also called Mt. Sinai in Exodus 3:1. In Hebrew the word Horeb means, "*Place of desolation.*" The barren environment perfectly matched the state of Elijah's soul. After a great victory for God, nothing changed in Israel. It was "business as usual" as people went back to their lives and their gods. People refused the revival Elijah was certain would result from the miraculous events on Mount Carmel. He felt discouraged and alone, an orphan. Yet this was God's mountain. Consider that the place we are in may look different to us than it does to God. To Him, the place of desolation and desperation is the place where issues of the heart are flushed out. It is a place where He shows up and shows His power.

Look at verse nine. Elijah is hiding in a cave when God comes to him and asks him a question: "*Elijah, what are you doing here?*" This is such an important question. We need to stop here and ponder our own lives. "*What are you doing in this place? Why did you come to this place called desolation? How did you get here? What do you want God to do for you?*" Elijah had come to the end of himself. He was desperate for God and came to His Mountain seeking Him.

In verse ten, Elijah revealed to God his orphan status.

> "*I have been very zealous for the Lord, the God of hosts; for the sons of Israel have forsaken Thy covenant, torn down Thine*

altars and killed Thy prophets with the sword. **And I alone am left;** *and they seek my life, to take it away."*

In 19:14, Elijah repeated this same statement again, even after God mightily showed Elijah His power and strength (19:11-13). Despite God's words and clues of His power, Elijah was still terrified and still felt like an orphan.

This was a new place for Elijah. It was not business as usual with God. In this place, God showed up differently than Elijah expected. God did not come to him in the wind, the storm or the fire as He usually did. He came to him in the still, quiet whisper as He revealed the lie in Elijah's soul:

> *You are not an orphan; you are not alone in the battle for Israel; there are others on the journey with you; I am not finished with you yet; I am with you; I will never leave you.*

In the rest of the passage, we see that God not only left a remnant of seven thousand prophets who still served Him, he sent Elisha to help Elijah. Elisha, a young prophet who would receive a double portion of Elijah's spirit (2 Kings 2:9) would walk with Elijah. Lies! Lies! Lies! Elijah was not an orphan and neither was I. And neither are you. Even Jesus Himself promised in John 14:18: *"I will not leave you as orphans."*

My Freedom Experience from Orphanhood

So, how did I get free? Once the Lord gave a name and exposed the spirit that was hidden in my heart, I was able to obtain freedom from it. Even considering an orphan spirit may not be part of your journey, we are all in bondage to something. Consider how these steps might help you get free in another area you struggle with. The Lord led me to take these steps, which took about a year and a half:

1) I began to pray and ask God to free me from what was holding me back in my writing and in other areas. I was

reminded of my grandmothers' journeys as I asked Him to take me back where this began. As each scene came to mind, I asked God to "break off" any agreement that I had made as a young person, knowingly or unknowingly, with the enemy that gave him a foothold into my soul. I asked God to break off any family agreements, curses or bondage made by my parents, grandparents or great-grandparents that were keeping me or my family down.

2) I forgave my great grand-stepmother for not wanting my grandmother. I also forgave my great grandfather for being weak and unwilling to stand up for his children. I forgave my father's grandparents for letting his mother go off to another country alone and unprotected. I asked God's Spirit to fill the now empty space in my soul, where orphan feelings formerly reigned, with more of His Presence.

3) I began to research the Biblical concepts of curses and bondage using reliable sources I learned about from trusted friends or trusted sources on the internet. I obtained some books that assisted me in my quest. I read some articles on the topic from pastors and others further along. I listened to sermons of trusted pastors who knew more than I did on the subject, both for and against the concept of generational bondage.

4) I learned to listen to my own words of negative self-talk. When I heard words that sounded like orphan words, I immediately repented. I asked God to give me a "check" to remind me when I was spiraling down. Now, in my head, I often hear the words, *"Don't go there"* and the words remind me to pull back under the shadow of His wings and take those wayward words and thoughts captive.

5) I set aside pride and went for prayer and counsel to others who were more knowledgeable in this area than I. I went to a trusted prayer room in the area with a specific request to pray for a breaking of the orphan spirit's grip on my life. I experienced some freedom through their prayers and I refused to go back to orphan thinking.

6) I began to reframe my childhood by asking the Spirit to take me back to areas where I had felt alone or abandoned. I took the memories I had and "reframed them" into more positive memories. I didn't change the facts like some in our culture try to do, but I reframed *my* thinking about what happened. For example, when I was five, we moved from Pennsylvania to California and I was forced to leave behind my favorite toys (a roll-top desk, a rocking horse and a toy kitchen), as there was no room or money to have them shipped. I have carried that pain for years. I reframed by asking Jesus where He was in that picture and seeing Him there with me to grieve the loss. I considered the journey my parents were about to take us on – a new adventure, a new life, new experiences all under the shelter of their wings. It helped me tremendously.

7) I read the Word, even more diligently than before. I was looking for promises and strategies. For some time, I wrote the promises and strategies on a white board at least one every day; then at week's end, wrote them in my journal.

8) I gave thanks to God over and over for revealing the deception. I asked His protection to keep me from entering into agreements like this with the enemy.

9) Don't be surprised if the issue arises again later in your life. Be prepared to deal with it with what you learn in Part Two of this book.

Beloved, we are treading in deep waters here and some of you may be reading this with an incomprehension that borders on fear. Or perhaps this may sound so foreign, so fantastic that you just cannot go here. Believe me, I understand. Just a few years ago, I was there. Had I not experienced these things in my own life or seen the victories that God desired to bring, I could not write about these things. Others of you may resonate with this story in a deep way as your own heart recognizes the journey. There is hope for us all.

Let me just share with you how Elijah's story came out (over many years). After Elijah's meeting on the mountain of desolation, God bestowed a double portion of Elijah's power on his mentee Elisha. Under that anointing, Jezebel was destroyed, Baal worship was abolished and a revival swept the northern kingdom. Elijah's call was not to lead a revival, but to prepare the way for one.

Finally, God does not bring curses on anyone. He sent His Son to break every curse and free the captives. The Cross breaks every yoke, no matter what we do or inherit. It is the enemy who settles on these things, hoping we never find out, hoping we never pray for the strength to break off these things for ourselves, our children and our children's children. As a praying parent, you stand in a place of authority in your children and grandchildren's lives to pray and stand against these things gripping your family.

This orphan experience would explain a lot about why I stepped out of the footsteps back in 2012. As I share my story with you, I'm going to show you actual words from my journal. You will see clearly the "orphan words" that led up to and caused me to move away from God and out of following His footsteps. Having shared this with other groups, I have seen that it is a powerful story because it touches on areas of sin most of us ignore. It's easy to spot the outward sins, but the attitude sins, the unbelief, disobedience, rebellion, pride – not so much. I had to learn the truth of the words, *"Whatever is not of faith is sin"* in a painful way. But I want you to see there is so much victory ahead, so much more that God wants us to experience with Him. He wants us to enter in, to see and know and accept that life is supernatural and joy and peace are available.

Chapter 9. Stepping Out - My Story

"Come to me with your ears wide open. Listen, and you will find life." -- Isaiah 55:3

"God loves me because He is He, not because I am I. Just like the sun shines on the earth, not because the earth is the earth, but because the sun is the sun." -- Pastor Mike Reed, Calvary Chapel Oceanside, California

Hidden Bondage

In *God's Smuggler*, Brother Andrew tells the story of his early days as a freedom fighter in the Dutch army. He was sent to Sumatra and there he purchased a gibbon (a species of monkey) as a pet. He had the gibbon for some weeks and it was happy and carefree. As it grew bigger, it became more and more downtrodden and apathetic. It lacked its prior enthusiasm and just moped around, very sullen. Andrew looked him over carefully and discovered that there was a wire wrapped around his middle that had not seemed to bother the gibbon when he was smaller. As he grew, the wire got progressively tighter cutting off circulation until he could barely breathe or move.

Andrew tells how one evening, with other soldiers looking on, he delicately cut away the skin to get to the wire. Though it was obviously painful to the gibbon, it continued to trust him and not thrash around. Finally, the wire was cut and the transformation was immediate! The gibbon jumped up and began to do cartwheels. Andrew tells how that reminded him of his own self and that he too was a captive until Christ came to set him free.

There was something in the gibbon's life that was unnatural to how he was meant to live. He was essentially in bondage to the wire encasing his body. He did not seem to be aware of it, nor did anyone else notice until a minute inspection was made and the wire was exposed. As the wire grew tighter, the gibbon grew more and more joyless and apathetic to life around him. It wasn't until someone with skill and understanding cut the wire that the gibbon was freed.

Sometimes we are like the gibbon – captive to something robbing us of joy and keeping us down, and we don't even know it! By our very nature, every one of us is in bondage to something, as we have already discussed. God wants to expose the hidden bondage, teach us how to "cut the wire" and set us free. Having recently experienced a "wire-cutting" in my own life, I know the feeling of being held down and, when freedom comes, of jumping for joy. Let me share with you how the wire sinuously wrapped itself around my life, constricting the life out of me. And then we will talk about how to cut the wire in *your life*.

"If only I had listened." That's the kind of looking-back, regret-filled statement I never wanted to make. God spoke, I heard, I responded but I didn't listen. Is anybody with me on this? Essentially the difference between hearing and listening is simply, "I hear it" versus "I get it." When God's Spirit warned me that I was about to step off a cliff, I heard Him and even wrote about what I was hearing, but did not respond or "get" what I was being told. The warning never registered and I failed to take steps to prevent the fall. It was a costly error. Sin is always costly – not just to self, but others in our world who are often touched with the consequences of our choices.

I have had a calling to write for most of my life. We have family pictures of me at age three with a pencil in one hand and a newspaper in the other. I wrote my first novel when I was twelve years old. It was a sappy 264-page romance, a cross between *Blue Hawaii* and *Gidget*. Don't wait for that one to hit the shelves any time soon! College professors urged me to write for a living. But I couldn't seem to make it happen, though I tried. I'm not sure why when I so clearly knew this was what I was supposed to do. I have written hundreds of Bibles studies and taught them; as an appellate lawyer, I have likewise written hundreds of briefs, but I could not seem to write the type of books I thought God was calling me to write. I have a shelf full of ideas. I *have* managed to get two Bible studies in print. But they were difficult to complete. I had joy in doing it, but it often felt like Sisyphus pushing a boulder up a mountain only to have it fall back down again.

I began to suspect that I might be experiencing some "hidden bondage" in 2006 when I was asked to teach a class on *Breaking Free* by Beth Moore. Once awareness came, I began to research, study and pray. I did obtain some freedom, but not enough to really break free. My pastor later asked me to write a series of sermon study notes for small groups while he was teaching through the gospel of Mark. I did so but shelved the notes, not even thinking of a possible book. During that time, in 2010, I got up my courage and went to a writer's conference in New Mexico. I was nervous about meeting editors and others who were in the field professionally. The leader of the newbies was a pastor named Ron Benson. He encouraged us to pitch ideas even if we didn't have a packet ready in writing. I felt an immediate nudge of the Spirit to consider the Mark sermon study notes I had written earlier. You never know when someone's words or actions can impact your life. Thank you, Ron.

I had contact with other editors who were enthusiastic to ideas I pitched. Almost as an aside, I presented the idea of writing a verse-by-verse study on the gospel of Mark to the one editor who was there from one of the few publishing houses that still publish Bible Studies. He was interested even though I didn't have anything in writing to give him. He asked to see a written proposal on Mark.

I went home from the conference very encouraged by the interest, but unfortunately, the voice of the enemy began to whisper, "*Your writing is nothing special. They ask everybody to send a proposal."* (Not true.) *"No one is really interested. You are wasting your time."* Those voices and life's messages coupled with my own insecurities paralyzed me for months. I finally decided to send a proposal to the Bible Study editor seven months later. I began writing the Mark study even though I didn't hear back from him. The study is an interactive, verse-by-verse guide through the Gospel of Mark filled with research, stories, analysis and interactive questions.[26] It took me over two years to complete. As I was writing, I experienced a deep flow of energy and joy. I prayed over every section. I was deep in the midst of Jesus' life with the disciples and I was walking with them too. I was writing a book *with God*, not just for Him. What I didn't realize then was that I needed to immerse myself in Jesus' life before I could make the journey up the mountain that I had no idea was before me. Writing the Mark study was an amazing though difficult journey.

As I wrote the Mark study, I had one specific prayer that I often prayed, *"God, use this book to reach people I will never be able to reach."* And I had NO IDEA how God took that simple prayer to His own heart or how much God really did want that book published. It was pretty normal as books go, but HE had a purpose. Not the purpose I thought, which is partially what derailed me later but just like every task He assigns, this book was important in His Kingdom.

When it was finally published, men and women were doing the study in small groups and some were being transformed. They were not just impacted, but changed from the core of their being as they came into contact with Jesus and the depth of His heart for them.

One young woman in particular who found her way to one of the studies was just coming out of the sex trade when she encountered Jesus face to face. His love transformed her from the inside out. She is now a speaker and consultant for law enforcement officials, schools and ministries, trying to help people trapped in that lifestyle. Police, judges and social advocates call on her for her counsel. While

I would not have a clue on how to speak to any of these groups (my legal training notwithstanding), she is confident she can help because it is her call to follow Jesus into that arena that she obeys. She credits the Mark study for pointing her to Jesus. I am deeply humbled by what happened to her.

I tell you this story to show you that you never know how God is going to use something He gives you to do or answer a prayer from the heart. Had I not written that study, she might still be in bondage. And remember my one prayer while writing the study: *"God use this study to reach people I will never be able to reach."* I had no thought at all that *this* would be how that prayer would be answered.

In my journey of writing the Mark study, God's plans were not clear yet, but isn't that just like Him to give you only a partial picture of the task at the beginning? This is a call to a deeper walk – requiring deeper trust and more obedience on our pathway. But the enemy has plans of his own too. God's plan for me was to stay the course, trust the outcome, and stay in the footsteps. The enemy's plan was to stop the presses, block book publication, and frustrate my efforts.

Shortly after sending off the proposal to the editor, in the summer of 2011, my husband retired. We sold our house and moved to a new area. It wasn't until about six months after moving that I contacted the editor again to inquire if he had reviewed the proposal. Surprisingly, he remembered the proposal and sent a very encouraging note back telling me how much he liked what he saw, how well done it was and, even if their publishing house didn't pick it up, that I should still go forward. He said he would take it to his team and get back to me. That was all I needed to mobilize. Someone in the field thought my writing was good. I began working on the book in earnest. I didn't hear back from him but he gave me the boost I needed to get moving.

Your Own Words Can Take You Out

For several months, I continued writing, but even during the process of creating with God, my wounded soul was stirring and I was having doubts. I wrote this in my journal in May, 2012:

> *"…I think now I'm in need of a watchman – to pray for the next step for me. In some ways, I feel an inner discouragement that I don't want to voice; that nothing will happen once the book is finished; that it will be 'all up to me', that God won't step in even though this is His work from His heart to mine or that somehow, I will be alone at the forefront of moving things along like I've always been in my family…"*

Okay. Let's stop here and evaluate. I was wise enough to see that I was in need of a watchman because the closer I came to actually finishing the book, the more the pain bubbled up and over. But I did not heed even my own words. I did not understand the tactics of the enemy to block me from doing what God called me to do. Nor did I think what I was doing was valuable enough to ask people to pray; I did not believe anyone believed that what I was doing was important. Why would anyone pray for me? Orphan thoughts, though at the time I had never heard the phrase. While I did confess the words on paper, I did not really understand the depth of what was in my heart. A very clear lack of faith is seen in these words, yet I did not see.

Let's look at the words. First of all, do you see the orphan words? Some of you may not have this issue, but look beyond the actual words to the sin embedded in the words. What do you see? I see for starters, lack of faith and doubt in God's promise to walk through this part of the journey with me; there was unbelief in the assignment I knew He had given me. I felt like He had planted me squarely in the middle of the desert and told me to get the job done. Period. It is a good thing I was not in David's shoes during this time. Goliath might have had my head rather than the other way around! And I want you to see that these are *my words* – not the enemy. The enemy is just an opportunist who will take our words, actions and attitudes to try and keep us on *that path.*

Because I had been a Christian so long and had such a long history of walking with Him, to have doubt was like a slap in His face. In this situation, for me, *doubt* was a sin. In Greek *doubt* means, *"to be without a way or without resources."* Was I without resources on my journey? Are you? God has given us numerous resources, some of which we will explore in Part Two of this book. In Greek *doubt* can also mean, *"To be perplexed, amounting to despair; to stand in two ways, implying uncertainty of which way to take."*[27] The word is used of believers whose faith is small (that hurts!). It implies a wavering between hope and fear. It can also mean to shrink back.

How could a leader in a church fall into this? I tell you so you can learn to be aware of what could be lurking in the darkness of your soul. All of us are susceptible, leader or not! Doubt rests in the shadows of the soul. One meaning is suggestive of stealth. Doubt says the promises are not for me. They must be for someone else. And behind doubt lurks shame, which causes us to shrink back even more from the light. Oh, beloved, there is healing to be had from these issues in the light of Jesus.

More Harmful Words from the Soul
Let's move on to the next section of the journal.

> *"…in my deepest heart, maybe I believe He can't be trusted to help me; that even though I am writing with Him, I'm still the one who has to make all the decisions…this is obviously a very deep place for me. This is why I'm not wanting to finish the book. I'm afraid nothing will happen. God forgive me for my lack of faith, my doubt, unbelief and independent spirit."*

Again, I was aware enough to see *something* and even ask half-heartedly for forgiveness. But I did not see clearly enough to move upon the words proactively. Nor did I sincerely repent of the words and attitudes behind them.

Because of my words, the enemy was poised to steal God's assignment from me and take me out. In the next chapter, I will unmask the enemy who comes to kill, steal and destroy.

Chapter 10. Unmasking the Enemy

"Be of sober spirit, be on the alert. Your adversary, the devil, prowls around like a roaring lion, seeking someone to devour. But resist him, firm in your faith, knowing that the same experiences of suffering are being accomplished by your brethren who are in the world." -- 1 Peter 5:8-9

"The devil…has a mirror of his own that he is continually shoving in our face. Unlike God's mirror, the devil's magnifies our faults and failures. It blows every imperfection out of proportion. It deceives, discourages, and destroys." -- Vicki Burke[28]

The Enemy Wants to Steal from You

When God gives us a task, the enemy has his own agenda with the full and direct goal of "taking us out." Jesus explained how the enemy does this by His words in John 10:10, *"The thief comes to kill, steal and destroy.."*. To "steal" comes from the Greek word *kleptos*, which means to "take by stealth." When you are not focused on Christ and walking in His footsteps, the enemy tries to steal from you without you knowing it. He tries to steal your peace, joy, hope and more. He wants to keep you blind to his activities in your life.

He also tries to steal your birthright just as he tried to steal Jesus' birthright in the desert. But Jesus was focused and taught us how to fight the thief. Understanding this is so critical to maintaining your relationship with Christ. If the first recorded thing the enemy did to Jesus was to grab Him and try to steal *His* birthright, you can be sure it is high on his list of areas to attack *in you*.

Your Birthright at Risk

The first thing I want you to understand is this: **The enemy *will* attempt to steal your birthright and calling.** An orphan himself after being cast out of heaven, the enemy does not fight fair. He does not care if you are an innocent child or a broken adult. He will use the traumas and wounds we experience to plant pain in our soul. If you are not freed from these things, they may fester and grow for the rest of your life unless you seek hard after freedom in Christ. You will not understand why you do some of the things you do. You will think, *"Everyone thinks this way."* and be surprised to learn they do not. You will develop habits and negative thinking or other things that seem to cling to you no matter what you do.

He will use those things and more to keep you out of following Jesus' footsteps by feeding you feelings of hopelessness and despair against the thought of ever changing. Or perhaps your pain is so deep you would never even consider putting your faith and trust in Christ because you (wrongly) feel He wasn't there for you when you needed Him most, at your most difficult moments. Lies, lies, lies! Hebrews 13:5 says, *"Never will I leave you; never will I forsake you."* You will end up blaming the wrong people or the wrong Person and not even see the enemy behind the scene orchestrating it all.

The enemy wants all of us to be orphans because he is one. He is a jealous and rage-filled foe who will stop at nothing to keep you from fulfilling your calling. If you are already walking with Jesus' (as in having put your faith and trust in Christ at some point in your life), the enemy will stop at nothing to neutralize you, keep you on the sidelines, pull you out of your calling and make you believe you are not God's beloved. But take heart. We have an even greater Ally. One who has walked in our shoes and now calls us to walk in His. The enemy tried to take Him out too.

Let's look at Matthew 3:16 through 4:11. Read it in your Bible, then let's talk.

70

The Birthright Given

At Jesus' baptism, the whole of the Godhead was present. The Spirit was present as a dove, the Son was present in His human body and the Father was present because we hear His Voice. After Jesus came up out of the water, the dove descended on Him (3:16) and in 3:17, a Voice from heaven said: *"This is my Son, whom I love; with Him I am well pleased." (NIV)* When God spoke those words from His throne-room, He was expressing to the world and to Jesus, His birthright. *You are My Son. You are loved by Me. I am very pleased with You.* These words infused strength, purpose and courage into Jesus' own soul to prepare Him for the way of His future while on earth. These words were spoken before Jesus even began His ministry. Jesus at that moment could have refused to do anything further and it would not have changed His Father's opinion at all. God breathes these very same words into us.

In Matthew 4:1, the very next verse, we learn that the Spirit led Jesus into the wilderness to be tempted by the devil. For forty days Jesus ate no food or drink and took the barbs and arrows slung at him by the enemy. Do you not think Jesus had His own pain growing up? Though He never sinned, He bore the stigma in that culture of being conceived before His parents married. Do you not think He suffered as He heard His mother being whispered about, His stepfather being laughed at behind his back? Even His later half brothers and sisters undoubtedly teased Him or rejected Him. Yet He bore the pain of rejection and is, in a way, an orphan too. He did not, however, let it settle into His soul, nor did He allow the enemy space in His soul. He never forgot Who He was and He never forgot the birthright the Father had given Him. Instead, Jesus wrestled with the enemy, teaching us how to do it by following how He did it.

He taught us three things:

1) Use the Word of God to fight your battles (Matthew 4:3-4).

2) Trust God to keep His promises (Matthew 4:5-7).

3) Worship God in every situation (Matthew 4:8-10).

After Jesus used these tactics, 4:11 says, *"Then the devil left him…"* If you get nothing else out of this book, mark this life-strategy well and make it your own.

Jesus' "temptation in the desert" was a series of three temptations designed to move Him away from the core of who the Father told Him He was:

> *"You are the beloved son." Not, "You are the one who can turn stones into bread; you are the one who can jump from the top of the temple and live; you are the one who can make others bow to your power."*

Yes, Jesus had authority to do all of those things, but that was not who He WAS. His identity was as the beloved Son of the Father. Satan tried to steal Jesus' core identity by giving Him a different identity. Jesus spent the whole of His earthly life living out "Who He was" according to the Father's heart and showing us how to live out our lives with the same core.

I knew "Whose I was," but I was also learning about "who I was" in Him. I am His beloved daughter, no matter what. My core identity is not, *'the appellate lawyer, the Bible Teacher, the one who keeps things going; the one who will make everyone's life run smoothly; the one who cannot finish what she starts."* You get the idea. Even when (especially when) I stepped out of the identity He gave me, God's opinion of me never changed. His compassion was touched. A rescue mission was set in motion from the throne room and His Spirit began to pursue me in ways I was, at that time, unable to see. His Spirit began to set before me clues and warnings to call me back. I still couldn't see.

The Enemy Wants to *Kill* You

Let's continue our review of John 10:10. To *"kill"* is the Greek word *thuso*. It means to "slay", *"to cover with smoke"*, to *"offer as a sacrifice by slaying the victim"*. The opposite word is *anazao*. It means, *"To flourish again; to live again; to revive and to preserve alive."*[29] Which would you rather have your life represent? A sacrificial offering of the enemy or a flourishing, revived, preserved person God can use for His glory? Notice the word, "again." That is an implication that we have already experienced a slaying of sorts. God can heal, resurrect and restore anything, including your wounded soul.

In your calling, in the tasks God gives you, the enemy will try to erect a smoke screen over you so that you cannot see God's plan, outcome or purpose. He does not want you to complete your God-given assignments. And if he could, he would kill you. But you need to remember and cement in your soul that God is with you and He has a plan. He will NOT allow you to be physically taken out until your purpose here has been completed. You are invincible until God calls you home. Hebrews 9:27 says our time of death *is appointed by God.*

If the enemy succeeds in putting a smokescreen over your calling, you will believe that nothing you say or do has any value, as in the following attack:

> *"No one will read what I write. Why do all this work? Everything has already been said and it is better than I could say it. It would be better not to waste time. Let it go."*

Let it go! These were phrases in the deep recesses of my life that battered my soul over and over again. And for years the words were successful. I heard how worthless I was and how nothing I could do would impact anyone's life and much more. I had to continually push through a darkness that often threatened to overwhelm me. I did not give up serving Him and using the gifts God had given me, but I

73

could hardly hear or receive God's words through others of how their lives were impacted through mine. I was unable to internalize those words, even though my words to others seemed to impact them. The enemy stole those words from me before they could take root in my soul.

Beloved, beware of these kinds of phrases being thrust into your life. It is one way you will know the enemy is desperate to keep you from seeing God's plan and moving forward in it. Reframe it and armed with that knowledge, keep moving forward. Stand firm. Never give up on what God has for you. His promises never die but you may need to wake up your soul to the truth of them in order to receive them.

The Enemy Wants to Destroy You

There are various Greek words for the word *"destroy"*. Listen to some of these definitions: *"to put out of the way; to render useless; to ruin; to pull you down; to cause someone to lose their will (not their life)."*[30] It can refer to salvation as in to cause someone to not be interested in the things of God. For those who belong to God, the idea is not to physically kill you but to do whatever it takes to ruin you, overthrow you, pull you down from your calling, move you out of the way, put you on the sidelines or make you lose heart for the journey.

I want you to stop here and ponder for a few minutes about the words Jesus gave us to help us understand what the enemy is trying to do to us:

- **Steal**: to take by stealth when you aren't looking; to steal your joy, peace, hope, family, physical life (stealing your health and finances), and spiritual life (stealing God's words and promises from you before you can fully own them).

- **Kill**: to slay, to cover with smoke, to offer as a sacrifice – covering your eyes with smoke (to blind you to what the enemy is doing and what God is doing) – and covering the eyes of others (to blind them from seeing your potential or how God could use you in their life or them in your life).

- **Destroy**: to move you out of the way; to render you useless by whatever means; to ruin you or your reputation, your health, emotional stability or cause you to lose your heart for God.

Do you see how understanding the meanings of these words brings light to the darkness that the enemy uses to cloak us? As you pray and ponder these words, jot down what the Spirit is saying to you about your own calling. Maybe your call is to raise your children in the Lord, stand alongside your spouse in his or her call, or step out into the flow of the culture and call desperate men and women back to Him. I do not know what He has called you to but I do know that, while every person's journey is different from mine, the battle is the same. It might not look like my battle, but if you belong to Him, you *will* be in a battle. We have a formidable enemy! But take heart, we have an even more formidable Savior.

In the next chapter we will take a look at another way the enemy operates to take us down.

Chapter 11. The Hidden Serpent Revealed

"Behold, I have given you authority to tread on serpents and scorpions, and over all the power of the enemy and nothing will injure you. – Luke 10:19

"The sin underneath all our sins is to trust the lie of the serpent [so] that we cannot trust the love and grace of Christ and must take matters into our own hands." – Martin Luther

Breaking a Lethal Fixation

I read a story a while ago about a young missionary in India who was riding his bicycle along a country road when he heard a ruckus in the trees with birds screeching loudly. When he stopped and looked around, he noticed a small bird on the ground trapped by the stare of a large cobra. By throwing a stone at the cobra, he was able to break the stare and the bird flew to safety.

The Serpent of Old

There is another way of looking at how the enemy strikes, which I have found to be very helpful in learning his strategies.[31] I am grateful to Dr. Michelle Corral for opening my eyes to how the enemy works in this manner. In 2 Corinthians 11:3 (NIV) Paul writes,

> *"But I am afraid that just as Eve was deceived by the serpent's cunning, your minds may somehow be led astray from your sincere and pure devotion to Christ."*

I wonder how many of us have thought about the enemy's wiles from this perspective?

The Stare of the Cobra

There is a reason why the enemy came to Eve as a serpent in Genesis 3. Eve was mesmerized by the stare of the serpent as he sinuously wrapped himself around her with words that transfixed her gaze. He used words that made sense to her, using her own thought processes to bring her to a deadly conclusion. Watch for that in your own life. Everything must be filtered through the Word of God and His Spirit speaking truth into your soul. Much as I did, Eve chose to filter what she heard from God through her own senses and thoughts: what she could see, taste and touch, rather than God's clear and explicit instructions. You have to actively listen and consciously choose.

The stare of the cobra not only mesmerizes you into a catatonic state, it also charms you. When I was writing in my journal, as you will see in the next chapter, what I was saying to myself made sense to me. I was just writing about the state of my own soul, trying to be honest. But what was happening was the enemy was using the words that made sense to me at that time to cause me to give up on what God had called me to do. I had stepped out of the footsteps into the stare of the cobra, which used my own pain and brokenness that was already resident in my soul. The enemy capitalized on my own thoughts to make me think it was the logical and sensible thing to do:

> *It's too hard. You're alone. No one will help you. You know this from past dealings that it's all up to you anyway. Why not give it a rest. Let this one go.*

Beware of the enemy who uses words like this to pour into your soul:

> *God has no use for you. He can't possibly use you. You are too flawed, too broken. Wait awhile until He fixes you.*

No, no, no, lies! These kinds of words advance the enemy's plans for you. They build onto your own thoughts to make you think that is what God thinks.

Let's stop right here for a moment and think on these things. Where are you in this? Are you feeling the pain of my words as they touch your soul? Do you see yourself in the stare of the cobra? If so, confess and cry out for deliverance. Help is on the way. Your part is to act on what God is showing you right now. Not tomorrow; not next week; not when you clean yourself up a little. Now is the time to cry out! You might want to stop here and write a prayer of your thoughts or feelings in your journal.

The Attack of the Adder (Asp)

An adder is a snake who holds his poison in his forked tongue. The enemy puts words in people's hearts and mouths to pull you out of your calling. A venomous tongue has taken more than one Godly person from his or her calling. I will show you an example from my life of what this looks like in the next chapter.

The Strike of the Viper

The strike of the viper is different from the adder. It hits when you least expect it. The snake waits under a bush on the roadside and as you are walking by, strikes out. It happens when you are not alert to your surroundings, not paying attention, distracted. It could be a financial strike, a loss of a job, a health situation, a betrayal or abuse or even depression that might overtake you. It could also be your own words, actions and attitudes that cause the viper to strike. You may be firmly walking in Jesus' footsteps when this happens. Your response to the strike can either take you out immediately or cause you to stand more firmly.

I experienced this so clearly one Sunday morning as I was about to deliver the closing talk of a three-day women's retreat. It was an important talk because it wrapped up everything we talked about the prior two days. It was a message of courage, hope and joy that the women (and myself) needed for the journey down the mountain.

My husband had just had surgery ten days before the retreat and was not yet recovered. I seriously considered canceling but the call was strong and both my husband and I had an assurance to go forward. That morning I called him just before sharing the final talk and asked how he was doing. Uncharacteristically he said, *"I'm not doing well. I feel pretty bad."* Strike of the viper! I immediately forgot all the plans that we had put in place for this contingency. Our son was home with him; one of our best friends, Richard Soikkeli, a deep prayer warrior stayed overnight. Neither of them had called to tell me things weren't going well. This is what I heard: *"He is going to die. You need to go home right now! If you don't go home, he will die and you will never see him again."* I heard that voice so loud and clear that I burst into tears after hanging up. And I had just taught about the strike of the viper the previous morning! I went into the conference room, grabbed my new friend Kelley Cua and some of the team and asked them to pray. The entire retreat went into prayer after that. I was able to deliver the closing talk only because of prayer! My soul became weary and weak at that time because I let the enemy sneak in and pull me out.

Nevertheless, after the retreat, I ran for home, ready to rush him to the hospital, only to find when I arrived that the three men were calmly sitting in our library enjoying a protracted time of prayer! I even tried to break up the prayer group insisting we leave for the hospital on the instant. All of this was based on the insidious words whispered to me earlier that morning. It was not until the next morning as I was praying that I recognized the strike of the viper.

Beloved, do not panic! Take the words immediately to prayer; be alert for the strike, fly to the shadow of His wings, and go to prayer until the crisis passes. Don't allow the words to make you give up your call, to cause you to act rashly or impulsively, or to think you don't even have time to pray.

The Squeeze of the Python

The python kills its prey by squeezing and suffocating it. As the victim tries to get free of the grasp, every movement toward freedom makes the python's grip tighter until the victim gives up. This would describe those of us who are frozen in depression, bitterness, anger or any host of other issues. It feels safer not to move because any movement to break the grip only feels more hopeless. The enemy banks on that, hoping you will give up your dreams, visions, hopes and callings. He tries to squeeze the life out of you. For years I was caught in his grip without being aware. I was like Brother Andrew's gibbon with the wire wrapped about him. But God had a plan of His own to break the grip. He always has a plan.

What we fail to understand is that when God says "go", the enemy says, "no". When God gives you an assignment, a task to do for Him, you can expect opposition. Not to expect it is to be ignorant of how things work. I was ignorant and missed the boat, but I'm adamant that you who are reading this and taking to heart the lessons I had to learn the hard way will be able to paddle around the shoals to victory.

God never, never, never leaves you alone to face the stare of the cobra, the attack of the viper, the poison of the adder or the squeeze of the python. He will always give you clues to make you aware of His presence with you. He will also give you clues and warnings of the evil one lurking on the fringes seeking opportunities to strike. In the next chapter, we will see how God throws some stones of His own to bruise the head of the snake, immobilizing him from overtaking our life.

Chapter 12. Warnings and Clues

"To whom can I speak and give warning? Who will listen to me? Their ears are closed so they cannot hear. The word of the Lord is offensive to them; they find no pleasure in it."
   -- Jeremiah 6:10

"Every past experience is preparation for some future opportunity. And one way God redeems the past is by helping us see it through His eyes." -- Mark Batterson

When Warnings Fail

Many ships leaving port from Southampton, England had reported to the Captain of the *Titanic* that icebergs were seen in the exact area through which the ship would be sailing. Twenty-one warnings were sent by Morse code to the Titanic by ships that had safely maneuvered the area. The warnings were sent over a three-day period between April 11 and April 14, 1912. Crew members also reported warning bridge officers of spotting possible icebergs ahead.

"Ice is a seasonal hazard in the unforgiving winter seas of the North Atlantic."[32]

It was neither unforeseeable nor unexpected. However, all the reports were ignored leading to the well-known consequences. Various statements I have read all agree there was no way the Captain and bridge officers could not have known about the icebergs ahead. The ship housed the finest communication equipment available at that time. There were communication officers on duty twenty-four hours a day. Nevertheless, the warnings were somehow, inexplicably, impossibly ignored.

Of course, that would *never* happen to you or me, right? History in particular and life in general are full of warnings and clues that we often miss. As you are reading this, perhaps other disastrous results from failed warnings came to mind. What about in your own personal life? Have you ever had a warning that you ignored to your detriment? This will be our chapter topic.

God Gives Warnings and Clues

Two days after the May 12, 2012 journal entry described in Chapter 9, God began to "throw stones" at the snake and the grip began to wane. Beloved, when you are about to fall, God gives clues and warnings that you can either heed or choose to ignore. However, our souls may be in a position where we are deaf and blind to the warnings. That was my situation. I could not see at all, but even in our blindness, He never leaves us without hope.

Hope is such an important word in His Kingdom. One of the Hebrew words for *hope* is *tiqvah*. It means "rope". God always gives you a rope of hope to hold on to but the enemy tries to steal the word from our vocabulary and our souls before it can take root.

That day I was out sitting on our deck to take in some of the sunshine and breezes the afternoon usually brings. As I was sitting, pondering and praying, two low-flying hawks flew by where I was sitting. They were so close, I could see the purposefulness in their eyes as they soared by and I felt the whoosh of their wings on my face. It reminded me of Isaiah 40:26-31. Turn there with me in your Bible and read the section. Make comments as you read.

> *O Jacob (O Kim)* **how can you say the Lord does not see your troubles?**...*have you never heard? Have you never understood? ... But those who trust in the Lord* **will find strength.**"

I knew it was a message from God but I didn't understand how important it was. I have recently researched hawks and I found this: Hawks are a bird of *prey*, p-r-e-y, or a bird of *pray* (as in prayer for increase and breakthrough, or prayer for victory, freedom). [33] It can represent a warrior able to overcome enemies who would like to take advantage of or make them their prey! The hawk was a promise and a warning. A bird of prey, *telling me to beware of the enemy who wants to take advantage of me, take me out or make me his prey.* And a bird of p-r-a-y to remind me to stay focused on Him and armor up for battle. I wish I would have known that back then!

That was God's clue coming to offer life and hope to my flagging spirit. It was also His warning. I saw the clue and missed the warning. The sighting did not solve my problem. The phone didn't ring with editors who heard about my book; no one was knocking on my door wanting to read the book. But, at that moment, He was with me and I knew it! And that is often how He shows up – in mystery, in the hidden, wanting to be found, but wanting us to watch for Him. It happens all the time. He does not answer our prayers in the way we think He should, but in some way, He reminds us that He is with us on the journey. But I missed His warning to pay attention.

After writing about this in the journal, I continued to trudge on through. I finished the Mark study on July 28, 2012 and once more, I was mesmerized by the stare of the cobra. I did not know what to do next. I half-heartedly tried to figure out how to publish the book. The more I researched, the more confused and overwhelmed I became, and the more angry I got at God. Let's look at how the stare of the cobra can take you out.

Five days after finishing the book, I wrote:

> *"I'm having a bit of a focus problem. My soul is wandering aimlessly…I know He is not finished with me yet, but I also feel devoid of energy, feeling and motivation. All of a sudden I feel done."*

Those unaccounted-for feelings may be a warning that the enemy is on the move. I am not talking about the everyday ebb and flow of energy. This energy drain was significant enough for me to write it in my journal. I needed to pay attention. It was time to go to prayer and go *for* prayer. But I still missed the warning.

The Enemy Can Use the Words of Others to Take You Out

The enemy's timing in what occurred next was masterful. The enemy can also use the pain of others to wound you and it can be toxic to your soul. When the enemy goes before the throne to accuse you, he will find no sympathetic ear. He will hear the words, *"Forgiven. Paid for at the Cross. Finished."* So the accuser instead turns to find a hearing among the fleshly ears of those vulnerable to criticizing others. His intent is to use words of criticism to his advantage and turn those words on us to take us out. They are words that touch our own pain and failure and contain a deadly strike to our calling. Watch for the attack and be ready to stand against it. Here is how it happened to me:

The same day I wrote the words above, the schemer used a college professor who is a good friend of ours. He is a beloved brother. He looked over the Mark manuscript and told us that it was well written with great insights but, *"No one will buy it. You are a woman and an unknown. Churches won't buy it because pastors don't know you."* The words made sense to me and seemed to confirm my own inner thoughts. Rather than rise up against those words and decry them for the lie they were, I agreed with them. I took them into my soul and it broke me. Beloved, none of those words were from God! Even if the words held some truth, God stands above the possibilities and even the probabilities. He is God. We are not. We must stay alert and stand firm. Pay attention to the Spirit's nudges in situations like this. It is always a mistake to take in negative words of others, no matter how kindly offered, unless the Spirit Himself prods you to the truth of them.

For example, if you are in sin and a brother or sister calls it out, then you need to listen. But what was said to me was not about my sin, *but about my call* and our friend's opinion on something God had instructed me to do. Do you see the difference? What I did was take a call from God to write the Mark study and instead of standing firm in *His* words, I listened to mine and someone else's words and let *those* words overtake the call God had on me. I had just received a one-two punch. My own words confirmed in a way by a good friend we looked up to, a leader in his field.

After this particular incident, the dominoes began to fall in my life. Words, which were not meant to tear me down, did. I took even the slightest inkling of doubt from anyone into my soul and made it my focus. Rather than stay true to the call God had given to me, I abandoned it – not openly, but I stopped trying. I was taken out, pushed to the side, overthrown just as the enemy had plotted. I am still dealing with the remnants of that strike.

Dr. Corral would call this a strike of the adder. I am convinced that our friend did not mean to harm me. I hold no anger toward him. He was just positing his opinion. Sadly, it was an opinion I secretly harbored and agreed with. In reality, though his words may have contained some truth to them, the effect on my fragile state was to pull me out of my calling. There are three important things you need to see when things like that happen to you.

Recognize the Instigator behind the Wounding Person

First, it is not usually the person who speaks the words who wishes to destroy you. The enemy lurking in the shadows wants to steal, kill and destroy. Keep in mind Miss Clara's words from the movie, *The War Room*. She could see more clearly what was really happening to Tony and Elizabeth's marriage. She told Elizabeth:

> *"Honey, your husband is not the enemy. The real enemy is Satan. He comes to steal, kill and destroy -- stealing your joy, killing your faith and trying to destroy your family. It's time for you to fight."*

Jesus gave us an example of this in Matthew 16:21-23. Stop here and read the verses; then let's talk. When He told His disciples what would happen to Him in Jerusalem, Peter took Jesus aside and reprimanded Him for saying such things. Jesus saw through the words to the instigator behind them. He turned to Peter and spoke directly through him to the enemy:

> *"Get away from me, Satan. You are a dangerous trap to me. You are seeing things merely from a human point of view, not God's."*

Jesus was quick to see that it was not Peter speaking.

If someone's words continually pull you down or cause you to doubt your call, it is time to go to prayer and ask for wisdom on whether this friendship needs to take a rest, be let go or confronted. If a spouse is the naysayer, continue in prayer until the Spirit speaks. He will answer any prayer!

The words of people we think love us cause the deepest pain. When this happens, consider the person and the words. People carry the weight of their own pain and baggage. In my situation perhaps this man's words reflected his own inadequacies because he hadn't written a book or maybe he wasn't feeling well that day. He may have been experiencing soul issues that *I couldn't see*. Henry Wordsworth Longfellow said,

> *"If we could read the secret history of our enemies, we should find in each man's life sorrow and suffering enough to disarm all hostility."*

Consider the Words

Secondly, ask for God's guidance here. Is there a sin you need to consider? If there is, receive the words and go immediately to repentance (See Chapter 23). Are these words trying to pull you out of the task God has appointed? If they are, do not receive them. We have to listen to both our own words to others and their words toward us.

Also, consider the response you made or should have made. I should have said something like,

> *"I know your words weren't meant for ill toward me, but those words go against the very assignment that God has given me to do. This is God's assignment and I cannot receive your words."*

Bless the Person whose Words Wound Us

Finally, even if you refuse to receive the words, pray an actual blessing over that person. This is personally challenging and counter to our natural reaction, but it is healing to our souls according to Jesus' statement:

> *"Listen, all of you. Love your enemies. Do good to those who hate you.* **Pray for the happiness of those who curse you;** *implore God's blessing on those who hurt you."* – Luke 6:27-28 (TLB)

Did you catch that part, *"Pray for the happiness of those who curse you?"* Implore God's blessing on the person? Is He kidding? Uh-no, He is not kidding. It is actually for *your* good that He gives those words. When you are obedient to the call to bless people, you will be blessed as well. Obedience and love are always shadowed with blessing. I should have immediately prayed a blessing over my friend. Consider this passage from Job 42:10:

> *"And the Lord restored the fortunes of Job when he prayed for his friends, and the Lord increased all that Job had twofold."*

It was not until after Job prayed for restoration of his friends, who by the way tried to move Job away from his place of calling, that God blessed him.

Beloved, most of us do these kinds of things all the time, not realizing how hurtful words can be to others *and their calling.* That is why words are so important – ours to others and theirs to us. We reap what we sow. If we sow words of blessing, praise and peace, that is what our lives will reap. Take it from one who is learning to step away from the power of negative words into the light of His presence. We need to be on the alert that we don't pull someone out of their calling by our careless words and that our own self-talk does not take us out.

Further, when someone else's words toward us have that effect, we must be ready to denounce the words, give them back to the sender and offer a blessing prayer for the person who said them. In *The Shelter of the Most High,* Francis Frangipane says,

> *"The accuser will feed words into your soul about who he thinks you are and who he wants you to believe you are or he will feed them to others to pour into your vulnerable ears. Beware…The purpose of God has been aborted in many Christians. Many who ought to be in awe of the Spirit of Christ within them have settled for a mere theology about Jesus Christ. Thus, Satan exploited their imperfections and buried their hope of Christ under a barrage of accusations."[34]*

Be alert for this kind of thinking: The enemy does not come to us with accusations that are without some small piece of truth, or in some cases, a lot of truth. He points out our lack of spirituality, our smallness. He exploits our ignorance and fears. He condemns us for our failures and our lack of interest in spiritual things. He reminds us of how much we do not know and our immature faith. Rather than give in to this kind of thinking, we need a defensive weapon. Here is where we remind the enemy of who we are in Christ.

> *"There is some truth to what you are telling me, but that is not who I am in Christ. He sees me clothed in His righteousness; He sees me as the beloved of God; He sees me completing the*

assignment He has given me and He sees the completion of the assignment fulfilling its purpose. He is doing a work in my life and I am holy and blameless before Him. I am redeemed and forgiven through the blood of Christ. I am His workmanship created in Christ Jesus for good works which God Himself prepared for me to experience. All that you accuse me of is covered by the blood of Christ and He Himself is working in me to bring about His glory." (Read Ephesians for more in this vein)

This would be a good time to stop and ponder your own life. Have you been captured by any such thoughts in your own soul? If so, write them in your journal and pray over them now, asking God to reveal to heal.

Biblical Examples

There are many examples in Scripture of people who were taken out or almost taken out of their calling by the words of others. Hezekiah comes to mind, as does Samson, Elijah, Job, Jeremiah and others. The one I want to call your attention to, however, is the apostle Paul. In Acts 16:14-18, after having led the first European convert to Christ (Lydia), Scripture records that he moved on and was headed to the house of prayer when he was confronted by a strike of the enemy. Stop here and read Acts 16:14-18.

Notice the setting here. Paul experienced a deep movement of God as Lydia the businesswoman and her household were saved and baptized. A strong house church would result from that experience. Now as Paul was about to enter into more prayer, an unfortunate servant girl who "had a spirit of divination" met them and began to follow Paul and his entourage. Notice the words she was using, *"These men are bond-servants of the Most High God, who are proclaiming to you the way of salvation."* There is a lot more to this story, which you will learn from my study, *The Acts Project*. What I want you to see is this:

91

While the words she used were true, they were inappropriate for that situation; they took away the focus from Jesus and placed it on the servant-girl. It was an attempt to distract Paul and the others from their call. It was also a dangerous ploy to confuse the hearers since the words she shouted were true and she was a known fortune-teller. Her words could create confusion for new believers. I also want you to think on these two things:

1) Beware of the enemy's deception. Even when demons spoke the truth about Jesus, He silenced them (Mark 1:23-25). Give no quarter to the enemy. We need to fine-tune our own spirit and soul to stay in alignment with God's Spirit.

2) Be very aware before you begin, after you have completed or are about to complete a God-ordained assignment. This is the vulnerable time when the enemy could come in striking as an adder or a viper. Learn how to protect yourself with the cloak of Scripture and the cover of prayer. Build a reliable prayer team.

God Sometimes Speaks through Dreams to Warn or Explain

Two days after the damaging words from our friend, I had a dream. The dream contained another warning and a clue. I dreamt that I was on a tour of a military installation. I know nothing about military installations. The place had trams you could take to different parts of the site where you would learn different elements of warfare. I got on a tram with two other people. The instructor was a specialist in tree warfare and hidden weapons. He was teaching us how to look at a tree to determine whether weapons were present. I am no dream expert, but I do believe God sometimes speaks to us in dreams. Those I remember, I try to write down in the journal for later analysis. In this case the analysis was too late.

Here's the analysis: The instructor, of course, was God. A tree represents someone with far reaching leadership abilities and strengths.[35] In this case, I believe this was my friend, a respected leader in his field. His words were a weapon used by the enemy to harm me. The Lord sent me a dream to warn me of taking in words of others without filtering them through what He had already told me or what I see in His Word. I did not understand the dream and beyond writing it down, I did not seek understanding. My soul was shrinking even more. And the enemy was stalking me, seeking to devour my faith.

In the next chapter we will explore a Biblical example about a prophet whose own words, attitudes and actions almost took him out!

Chapter 13. The Man Who Stepped Out – A Biblical Warning

"Be careful that you do not refuse to listen to the One who is speaking. For if the people of Israel did not escape when they refused to listen to Moses, the earthly messenger, we will certainly not escape if we reject the One who speaks to us from heaven!" – Hebrews 12:25 (NLT)

"To what will you look for help if you will not look to that which is stronger than yourself?" – C. S. Lewis[36]

A Biblical Example

There are lots of Biblical examples of God sending warnings through dreams and other ways. In Matthew 2:12 the wise men were warned in a dream not to return to Herod to tell him where the Child was. The very next verse, 2:13-15, tells us that an angel came to Joseph in a dream to take the Child and flee to Egypt. God chose Jesus' earthly mother and stepfather very well, I think, don't you?

But the story that keeps coming to mind as I pray over this chapter is the plight of Jonah. If you have ever been in a church Sunday school class or loved *Veggie Tales*, I know you're familiar with this story. But if you're not, it is a short story – four chapters in the Old Testament. I would like you to stop and read Jonah 1-4 before moving on. I so relate to this story in my own journey. I think many of you will too.

Jonah was a prophet of God during the reign of Jeroboam II, king of Israel. He ministered at the same time as the prophet Elisha. Some Hebrew traditions teach that Jonah was the son of the widow of Zerephath who was raised from the dead by Elijah (1 Kings 17:8-24). We first meet Jonah by name in 2 Kings 14:25. He had a zeal and a love for Israel his country. You might call him a patriot. He boldly prophesied that land stolen from the Assyrians (of which Nineveh was a part) would be restored to Israel.

Nineveh was a great city, but was known for its cruelty and graphic treatment of captives. Its modern day location is near the city of Mosul (Iraq). There were many mentions in the Bible of Assyria harassing surrounding nations including Judah and Israel. They made repeated raids into neighboring kingdoms demanding tributes, capturing and enslaving people and bullying kings. Eventually Israel of the divided Kingdom went into Assyrian captivity (while Judah many years later went into captivity in Babylon).

The story begins when God gave Jonah the assignment to go and preach to Nineveh (Jonah 1:1-2). Instead, Jonah turned and ran in the opposite direction. It was approximately five hundred miles to Nineveh from where he was and instead he traveled two thousand miles in the opposite direction to Tarshish (modern day Spain). It was Jonah's hard-heart, doubt, unbelief, disobedience, anger and bitterness peppered with some guilt and maybe fear, that sent him fleeing from God's presence. As if he could ever flee from God's presence.

He did not like Nineveh, did not want to go there, and did not want God to speak to them. Jonah experienced a warning – some call it a consequence when he was dumped over the side of a ship in the middle of a raging storm. But God arranged to save Jonah by having him swallowed by a great fish, where he lived for three days. During that time, in chapter 2, we see that he got his attitude somewhat straightened out and somewhat repented of his actions, attitudes and words. Then in Jonah 2:10, *"The Lord commanded the fish, and it vomited Jonah up onto dry land."* Well, that is pretty graphic! I am happy to report that my warnings were not quite as striking or drastic as those Jonah experienced.

In Chapter 3 the God of the second chance came to Jonah again commanding him to go to Nineveh with a message that, *"I will tell you*" (Jonah 3:2). This time Jonah obeyed but was still grudgingly obedient. He did not know the message. Perhaps it was God's grace to Jonah not to tell him. Had Jonah known that he was to preach good news, he might have continued in his disobedience, perhaps requiring a stronger warning!

To his surprise (and frustration), the message God sent was one of grace and mercy. The city heard, believed, repented and obeyed. Jonah was not happy. He hated the Ninevites and what they were doing to his beloved Israel. He would have much preferred God's judgment not His mercy to fall. In Chapter 4, we see Jonah sitting under a tree whining and complaining to God, and the story ends with God's question to Jonah, "*...should I not have compassion on 122,000 people who do not know...?*"

I relate to Jonah in a painful way. God gave me a task to write a Bible study on Mark, which I did joyfully – in the beginning. But when God's silence as to how to get it published continued, I became just like Jonah: whining, complaining, bitter that other people had more favor than I, doubting His presence and His assignment. Oh, yes. I sat under the tree too. But I want you to see this: God still works. He can use people who do not want to be used by him. God can use people who are reluctant. God can use people who are blind to His movement in their lives. Beloved, God can use anyone in any state of mind for any purpose of His. But that does not mean He always will do so or that the person being used will find any joy in it. His purposes for us may become flawed by our own choices. We cannot experience the delight, joy, light, love and breathtaking wonder of being in His Presence. Surrendering to Him and joyful obedience are for our own good. I was pretty miserable and, my guess is, Jonah was too!

It is a good thing Jonah obeyed God the second time, even grudgingly. Did you notice as you read the story that everything and everyone else in the story showed instant obedience to God's call? The wind, the worm, the fish, the sailors, even the renegade and cruel Ninevites listened, and obeyed! Jonah was the lone abstainer in the story.

There are times when it is necessary for God in His love and mercy toward us to send more warnings and clues that we are stepping out in order to bring us back into the footsteps. That was my journey. As I failed to pursue the next step in the journey, publishing the book, I had a more disquieting warning. One that had me scrambling to obey! I will tell you about it in the next two chapters.

Chapter 14. When Warnings and Clues are Not Enough

'For when I called, they did not answer. When I spoke, they did not listen. The deliberately sinned before my very eyes and chose to do what they know I despise.'' – Isaiah 66:4b (NLT)

"The essence of sin is disobedience to God. And disobedience to God is automatically obedience to Satan, God's enemy." -- Dr. Charles Kraft

Failed Warnings

In the late 1800's the town of Johnstown in western Pennsylvania was a modest but thriving community. The prestigious South Fork Hunting and Fishing Club was situated fourteen miles outside of town. Boasting such venerable members as Andrew Carnegie and Andrew Mellon, the Club restored an abandoned earthen dam to create a pleasant lake for its members. It stocked the lake with expensive fish for their fishing pleasure and served as a sailing lake in the summer and a winter sports lake in the winter.

Some Johnstown residents were concerned about the dam's safety since it had been abandoned before for structural issues. Daniel Morrell, a civic leader in the town, had the dam inspected and the investigation revealed major and serious flaws, which were pointed out to the Club. The Club summarily dismissed those warnings, which left some residents feeling the Sword of Damocles hung over their town. But because the town received warnings at least once a year, many people became immune to the warnings, believing, even if it did break, no more than a few feet of water would reach them doing little or no harm to the town.

In May of 1899 after several days of heavy rains, the Club members became aware of serious dam erosion. Screens added to the emergency spillways by the Club to stop their fish from escaping were clogged with debris. There was little the Club could do now. They sent a warning to the town, but it was ignored as being just one more false alarm over many years.

Inevitably the dam burst, propelling twenty million of tons of debris down the fourteen-mile path, leveling the town, and killing 2200 people.[37] The warnings and clues given to both the Club and the townspeople were largely ignored resulting in a cataclysmic consequence.

One of my closest friends, Connie Gilbert was born in Johnstown. As a young girl, her great grandmother told her stories of the "great flood." As a survivor of the tragic event, she was able to give Connie an eyewitness account of how warnings were given and mostly ignored.

Later in this chapter we will read a story from John 5 in which Jesus warns a man the day He heals him, and warns him again the following day even more strenuously. What you and I do with the insights (warnings) gained from this Bible reading can change the course of our own history. But first let me tell you how I came upon John 5. Clearly, God was trying to communicate with me.

The Enemy Gains Footholds into Our Souls by Our Attitude

As we take one last look at my journal, I want you to look for the *orphan* words and the sin words. And remember this took place three years before I ever heard the words "orphan spirit" in relation to my life. Look for words revealing a flawed perspective, or debilitating words accepted as the truth, but that are clearly lies.

Even, and sometimes especially, church leaders, people who lead ministries, pray over others, teach thousands of others year after year can completely miss the mark. How is this possible?

Believe me, if I didn't think that every one of you reading this has the potential to do exactly what I did and more, I would not be writing this. Who wants to share their "mess-timony", as Donna Partow calls it? Who wants to talk about arrogance, pride, rebellion, disobedience and more unless they are talking about *someone else!* Why would anyone who wears a tiara and holds anointing oils of healing in their heart want anyone to see the darkness inside? I've had to ask myself this question a lot. Two reasons come to mind: Because He asked me to share this and because you need to hear you're not the only one:

> *You are not an orphan; you are not alone in this journey; there is hope for your future. He is with you and, if you are willing to surrender and work with Him, He will do mighty works of rescue and freedom in your soul too!*

Your inner self-talk can change your attitudes, influencing how you see. I had been negative in my thinking for so long that I believed it was normal. *That's just how God made me.* No! No! No! I was made to give glory to His Name, praise Him, exalt Him, and to enjoy a creative, abundant life with Him. And so are you. I want you to do two things as you read the next journal entry:

1) Highlight the sin words/attitudes you see.
2) Highlight the orphan words that you see.

The journal entry was written in 2012, five days after the hawk sightings mentioned in Chapter 12:

> *"I realize, like a petulant child that I'm angry at God. Angry because I don't feel like or am not experiencing life as the favored child. All my issues are cropping up again, as God knew would happen: The one not picked, not favored, not chosen. I am feeling even more dangerously broken than ever. I go through the motions...I'm trying to converse normally with God, but I'm petulant, sulking, wanting to walk if not run,*

but there is nowhere else to go. Where could I go from Your Spirit? I knew once I wrote the book, that this place would be waiting for me, which is why I was so reluctant to finish it. I had to drag myself through because I knew I would be entering the silence where all my old lies would surface – like addictions never conquered. I think they can never be silenced or vanquished, though in reality, according to the Word of God they are. But I think they are not, so I let them creep back in, and if not take up residence, at least squat long enough to bring me grief. Then, when I picture myself vanquishing them with my sword, I picture myself...not God, not Jesus, not even His Word. I picture me...more isolation and weakness. I am weak, tired and there is no one to talk to...no one to help me crawl out. So like the most dependent, weak, helpless addict, I lie here – like the lame man at the Bethesda waterside. I watch as others are drawn into the water and walk out healed. And I am the one still here. (John 5:1-15) And, where did that Bible story come from?" [Ouch!]

Before we talk about John 5, I want you to see my attitude and the state of my soul. Sometimes it is easier to see someone else's sin and ignorance than your own. I put myself out here for you so you can see more clearly and use my story to bring yours more clearly into focus. Your choices, experience and journey will be different, but some of the attitude sins I engaged in you have too. Circumstances may differ, but the sin is the same. Are you with me on this?

Taking a Closer Look

So, how did these attitude sins reveal themselves? Clearly, there is anger, insolence, envy, rebellion, and I think some bitterness, unbelief and pride. As you look at these words think about your own life and how some of these attitudes may (or may not) play out in your soul. What other things do you see?

I was angry with God because of His failure to love me or care for me. Is that a true statement? Has He *ever* failed to love me, you or anyone else? No. So the statement was a lie. But, even though it was a lie, I was still left with that feeling resident in my soul, and it was fed by my failure to see, confess and repent.

I want to stop here for a moment to see the interplay between sin and emotion here. What emotions do you see in the sample above?

According to *Unger's Bible Dictionary*[38] **anger** is,

> *"an emotion of instant displeasure or indignation. It arises from the feeling of injury done or intended...anger is a sin when it is transferred from the guilty (me) to the innocent (God)."*

In a way, anger is no more than an unmet expectation. I expected God to miraculously open doors to publishing agencies, but, along with that, I did not have the faith necessary to open those doors.

Insolence

Insolence shows up in my attitude throughout the reading: *I knew this would happen; I knew He wouldn't help me; Why would He care about me?* The word comes from the Greek word *enubrizo*, which means to treat insultingly, or with disdain toward a superior.[39] Can you imagine treating the God of the universe in such a way? Unfortunately, people (including us at times) do it every day.

Envy

I was clearly *envious* of other authors who I perceived had it easier than I did. And I knew nothing about their journey. **Envy** comes from the Greek word *phtonos*. Lawrence O. Richards[40] says that it is a bitter feeling roused by what someone else has that we want. *Ungers* calls it a "detestable vice."[41] Yes, I wanted what they had. I was unhappy with how God was working in my life.

Rebellion

The entry also contains a strong flavor of *rebellion*. I had a rebellious attitude – which goes along with insolence toward God.

According to Richards, *rebellion* is the refusal of a servant to carry out his responsibilities; an attempt to void the relationship. It means to be hardened; determined not to respond to God. I never imagined I was harboring such rebellious attitudes. If I had recognized it, I would have immediately have done something about it.

Bitterness

I have always feared having a *bitter* heart; so to see it resident in the words that I wrote caused me deep pain. How did I get to this place? Was it possible to receive healing? (Yes) Richards says the Greek words for bitterness mean, *"To cut, prick, sharp. A root of bitterness produces bitter fruit."* It can also mean to be toughened. In the New Testament, the word has to do with a bitter taste. It focuses on,

> *"An angry and resentful state of mind that can develop when we undergo troubles...the New Testament reveals bitterness to be an angry, hostile outlook on life."*

Bitterness can toughen you, but not in a good way – a way that leaves you ironic, sardonic, hardened and unbelieving. Take heart, there is a Healer who desires nothing more than to set you free.

Pride

Michael Mangis in his book *Signature Sins* calls pride a signature sin or a root sin, one that overshadows other sins. It is the opposite of humility. I had (and still have) pride. So do you. God hates pride because of what it does to us. It makes us ugly, grasping, and critical. The word *pride*, according to Richards, is an attitude that draws us away from godliness. The Hebrew word *zid* means "self importance" which leads to acts of rebellion and willful disobedience. The Hebrew word ga-ah refers to an arrogant insensitivity to others, *'matched with overwhelming self confidence that leads to destruction.'* The root of pride is a refusal to consider God or respond to Him. It is a denial of Who He is and who we are in His kingdom. The New Testament word *physiosis* speaks of the inner impact of pride on the soul. It makes us conceited and puffed up and is tied with jealousy, anger, slander, gossip and quarreling. (2 Corinthians 12:20). You can see some of those words tied in with my journey from my journal.

Unbelief

I will tell you, however, that the sin of *unbelief* was the sin that grieved me the most when I was reviewing this journal entry two years later. It is not just a lack of faith. It is the opposite of faith. Mounce[42] says that it can impede or stop the miraculous from occurring, using Matthew 13:58 as an example of the use of the word. *"And He [Jesus] did not do many miracles there [in Nazareth] because of their unbelief."* My unbelief was holding me back. No wonder miracles were so sparse in my life then.

Okay, so let's stop here and review the words above and their meanings. Do any of the words explain any feelings or thoughts you are experiencing or have harbored in your heart? If so, jot them down now and pray over them, repenting, asking forgiveness and receiving cleansing. I will be giving you more help on repentance, cleansing and forgiveness in a later chapter, but for now, bring these attitudes to the throne, confess them to God, receive His forgiveness and leave them there.

In the next chapter, we will explore the Bible passage that had me scrambling to obey.

Chapter 15. Failed Warnings -- A Biblical Illustration

"Stop sinning or something worse may happen to you." – John 5:14 (NIV)

"Like it or not, sin has consequences. Which is why God lovingly warns us against it. Thankfully, He is merciful and ready to forgive if we ask Him. But that doesn't erase natural consequences of our actions. Cause and effect." – Julie Klassen

A Biblical Story: the Man who Failed to Follow

As I mentioned earlier, there may be times in your life when you fail to hear or heed God's clues and warnings. At times He might choose to hold us a little tighter, causing us to have to take note. That was what happened to me when I prepared to shelve the book after those disastrous words from the journal coupled with the words from our friend.

Let's take a look at how God used a story of deeper consequences from His Word to startle me awake. There are times when warnings and clues are not enough. When the story of the lame man at the Bethesda pool came to my mind, I knew it was God speaking again. It was not the message I was hoping for. I never even really liked that story! Let's stop here and read John 5:1-15 in your Bible, then let's talk.

In John 5:1-3, as Jesus returned to Jerusalem for one of the holy days, He passed the pool of Bethesda, which in Hebrew means *"house of mercy"*, and in Greek it means *"house of grace"*. A multitude of sick people, including the lame, blind and paralyzed sat there day after day hoping for healing. They were sitting in the house of mercy and grace and very few of them received either.

Verse four is not in all of the Bible manuscripts, but the verse says that at certain times an angel came to stir the pool. The actual word for pool in this section means, *"A deep pool from underneath that comes up bubbling"*. Maybe it was an angel, or maybe it was an underground spring. Whatever or whoever it was, the event happened and apparently the first person into the pool when the stirring began was healed. Had that not been so, people would not have waited year after year to be the first in.

I think it is interesting that in John 5:5-7 Jesus saw the crowds of sick people. He could have healed them all in an instant. Instead, He focused in on one man who was probably toward the back of the crowd. We also learn that the man had been there thirty-eight years. As Jesus approached the man, He did not introduce Himself but got right to the point, *"Do you want to get well?"* Notice that the man did not answer the question. We do not know if he wanted to get well or not. Unlike me who was screaming, *"Yes, I want to get well!"* Or so I thought. At that time I was unwilling and probably unable to do what was required for healing. I had to experience the painful consequences of walking without a sense of His presence and getting desperate before surrender and healing came. The man had an excuse too. In verse seven he said,

> *"There is no one to put me in the pool. Someone always get there before me."* (Versus) *"Other authors get publishers. I am the only one who does not have one. There is no one to talk to. No one to help me crawl out of this mess I am in, no one to help me get in the pool."*

Do you hear the orphan words here? Do you see the parallels? In other words, *"I am an orphan, I am weak, I am helpless, I am alone, I have been abandoned to lie here in the house of mercy and grace. No one cares about me."* And Jesus was standing right in front of the man. Beloved, there are times when Jesus stands before us with arms open, ready to heal and embrace and we are covered in so much darkness that we do not see. The lame man could not see. I could not see either.

Then the man told Jesus, *"Every time I try to get in, someone gets in before me."* That sounds like failure, doesn't it? Thirty-eight years of trying and failing.

As we come to verse eight, I want you to notice something. Jesus did not enable the man to enter the pool. He did not pick him up and tenderly place him in the pool. The man was so focused on getting into the pool I think he might have lost his way. The *pool* became the central focus of his life, his idol. Jesus did not put that man in the pool because Jesus did not want him to believe the lie that being first in the pool would make him well. Secondly, Jesus knew that putting him in the pool would not help him. Jesus wasn't interested in enabling the man to be first in, to be at the top. Jesus' purpose was to take him completely out of the competition, to empower him with God's power. In my case, I believed the only way to get a book into the stream for others to read was to have a traditional publisher do it. That turned out not to be the case.

After Jesus heard the man's sad story, He made no other comment about the man's plight. Instead, in verse eight He told the man three things:

1) **"Get up."** The word in Greek is *"egero"* which means, *"rise, wake up, be resurrected, lift up your eye"* It can also mean to wake up from lethargy or rise up against an adversary. That got the man's attention. He instantly stood up even though he did not know to Whom he was speaking. There is power in Jesus' words.

2) **"Pick up your mat."** Jesus didn't just tell him to get up, He told him to get up and take his mat with him. He was not letting the man leave a safety valve behind. He was not to leave his bed there in case the healing did not work. Jesus was

giving the man every opportunity to make no provision for failure. No more bondage.

For me the mat was the book. I was to make no provision for failure. Just get it published! For you it could be anything in your life. Stop now and think about your own "mat." What is it in your life that you need to make no provision for failure? What strongholds or addictions are you holding on to that you are afraid to give up because Jesus might not be there for you? What things do you hold on to, "just in case"? Jesus will not fail you if you trust Him. Jesus empowered the man by telling him he had the strength not only to pick himself up, but to pick up his mat too.

3) *"Get up, pick up your mat* **and walk."** A synonym for **walk** in this section actually means to *"follow"*. Jesus is telling to man to, *"Follow Me – get in My footsteps."*

No one is going to carry you except Jesus and there are times when, while He is with you, He will not pick you up. He wants you to choose to follow Him. He wants you to put your armor on (more of this in a later chapter), stand firm and fight alongside of Him. We think we need help: *"Who will mentor me, who will counsel me, disciple me, pray for me, teach me, study with me, help me with my kids? Who will publish my book? Who will market it"*? Me, me, me. When we get in the "me-zone", we are out of the "God-zone"!

Part of the message Jesus was giving this man is the message of making no provision for failure. You might be living in a miserable marriage, addicted to something, have problems with your children, or have issues moving forward. Maybe you have a tendency to lie, gossip, get angry too easily. Whenever you find yourself in a situation where you find it hard to move, get in the God-zone. Listen to Jesus' words, *"Get up, take up your mat and follow me."* That's where the help is!

I was out of the footsteps in unbelief and negative thinking. Beloved, I was addicted to negative thinking for so long that I felt as helpless as the most confirmed addict! That was my addiction. For me, coming out of it was a process. It was no instant healing but a day-by-day, moment-by-moment crawl in His direction. I did not know how to overcome it on my own. And I still battle it, though with more understanding and freedom.

Indeed, no self-improvement program could have changed that in me. It had to be wholly a work of His Spirit alone, in me. I had to cooperate with His Spirit to get free. But at that time I was not following, listening or applying the healing words of Scripture to my situation. I was in rebellion and I thought it was all up to me. I was in the me-zone and I was food for the enemy. I want to remind you that Jesus went to that man – chosen out of all the others to tell him to follow and make no provision for failure. Are you hearing Him speak into your own life as we read this story? The story is there to teach us to listen and obey.

Sneak Attacks and How They Can Take You Out

Okay, let's pick up the story at John 5:9-13. Here is another example of how the enemy works through others. We have already looked at how others' words can impact you. Here, when questioned by the religious leaders, the healed man had no idea who had healed him, for Jesus had slipped away into the crowd and the man failed to follow. And now the man will face his first opposition – alone, unprotected and out of Jesus' footsteps. Notice the timing: it was the same day. Shortly after leaving the house of grace and mercy he was put upon by the opposition. Before he even had a chance to evaluate what had just happened, he met up with the enemy who was at work behind the man's critics. The enemy never gives you a chance to gather your wits. When you go even a step or two of heading in the right direction, he goes on the immediate attack, which is why you cannot rely on your own skill or confidence to battle with him.

Paul emphatically informs us that our weapons of warfare do not come from the flesh (2 Corinthians 10:3-5). Let us realize this now: We cannot fight the enemy on our own with our own skills, talents, or self-confidence, no matter how great we may think they are. Fighting the enemy is a work of the Spirit in us as we cooperate with Him and learn how to use the weapons He has given us. Part Two of this book is dedicated to exploring some of those weapons and learning together how to put them into practice.

The enemy responds using the words of men, *"You can't carry your mat on the Sabbath. You can't be healed on the Sabbath."* Or in my case, *"You can't publish a book by yourself. You can't market a book without a publisher."* Beloved, when God gives you a task, He always empowers you to perform it and fulfill it. Our responsibility is to obey!

The next day in John 5:14-15 we see the serious warning, *"Stop sinning!"* I was to crawl out of my lethargy and do what God had already told me to do. I thought as I read, *"What sin?"* At first glance, I did not see any sin in the man. But the inference here is that his failure to follow Jesus as instructed was sin. The warning was clear. There was no happy reunion, no high-fives, no reminisces over the healing. Just a warning. The man had a choice: obey Christ's command or go his own disobedient way.

In John 5:15 Jesus warned him of the consequence of future disobedience: *"It may go worse for you."* We do not know what happened to the man. He made no response to Jesus' warning. We have already seen from Scripture that God will give us clues and warnings. Jonah's failure to obey took him through a slide into the belly of a sea monster!

I finally recognized my marching orders (and the implied discipline to be expected from non-obedience). Since I did not want things to go worse for me, I picked up my book and hired a subsidy publisher, taking money out of our savings on the strength of my husband's resolve and the tattered faith I had managed to salvage. A few

112

months later, I had a copy in my hand and I began the harder part of the journey -- marketing.

We cannot take lightly our counter-action to God's commands. Jesus called it sin. Jesus healed the man out of His love for him, but even with the healing, the man had free will to follow or not. Jesus gave him a warning to stop sinning or something worse might happen. It could not be clearer. During the next two years after publishing the book, I had many God-sightings:

- People came into my life wanting to help.
- People wrote me that they were blessed and changed.
- My husband valiantly assumed the role of editor, drill sergeant, and personal counselor.
- I was invited to speak to groups at different churches, retreats and Bible studies.
- In its beginning, over 400 people studied the book and many testified to being deeply touched and even changed in their souls by learning to walk intimately with Jesus through the Gospel of Mark.
- A group of women who went through the study in the spring, wanted to do it again the following summer because of things they might have missed. The message of the book stayed with these women over a year and a half and was still simmering in their souls. Who does a Bible study twice when there are so many good ones out there? These were all messages from God's heart to mine.

In all these blessings I would experience elation and give praise to God, but the encounters would fade after a day or two, almost like they had never happened. I was ignorant of the dealings of the enemy at that time. I did not know that he was robbing me of God's goodness and encouragement.

Unfortunately, rather than the blessings and encouragement, the negative seeds planted by others and me took root. For the next two years, even as I marketed the book, spoke to groups, facilitated the study, there was a deep place in my soul where I went into negative thinking, depression, discouragement and despair. The things I had written about in the journal stayed with me. I did not repent, nor did I recognize my words, attitudes and actions as sin. Most of this was not visible, even to me. These were things I was struggling with deep in my soul. I still looked pretty good on the outside. God was even still using me, but on the inside, I eventually realized something was desperately wrong.

Beloved, we are walking in deep waters again when we consider our words, attitudes and actions and how they impact everything around us. But praise God that He is a loving and merciful Judge; an Advocate who will never sleep; a Shepherd who will never leave; a Savior who will forever rescue and deliver! If you have fallen into these deep waters alongside of me, He calls us out beyond the waves to the river of life. As Dory from *Finding Nemo* would say, *"just keep swimming."*

Next up, we will begin to unravel how this upheaval in our souls happens. We will see how we make contracts and agreements with the enemy and how our cooperation with his plans can keep us out of experiencing God's abundance. And, of course, we will talk about how to break off those agreements.

Chapter 16. Making and Breaking Contracts with the Enemy

"Above all else, guard your heart, for everything you do flows from it." -- Proverbs 4:23 (NIV)

"There is a battle, a war and the casualties could be our hearts and souls." -- Ken Gire

Legalistic Intimidation

The first day of law school is usually a memorable experience. Most lawyers and non-graduating law students remember it well. I started law school at night because I worked during the day. All first-year law students start with a Contracts class. I was already nervous about attending as was every single one of the seventy plus students in the class that night. For once, we were all on time and seated before the Professor entered the room. We had read and attempted briefing some fifty cases for the first class meeting. When the professor walked in to the room, he did not speak. Although I can't remember his name, I remember what he was wearing – a three-piece brown/orange colored suit. He had red hair and a red beard. He was not tall, but he was mighty. The force of his personality burst into the room and every one of us came to attention.

The first words out of his mouth were, "Is (John Doe) in the room?" I cannot remember the unfortunate man's name. Thinking perhaps he had a message from home or maybe he was being singled out for some honor, the man jovially spoke up, "Here. I'm here." Without further adieu, the professor said, "Please stand and recite the case of *Lucy v. Zehmer.*" It is significant that out of the thousands and thousands of cases I have read since that fateful evening, I still remember *that* case. The man stood and haltingly tried to "cite" the case. None of us even knew what that meant.

For the next ninety minutes, the professor had the lowly worm on his hook. Nothing the student said was right; everything was questioned, drilled, screamed and hammered at the man. There was very little teaching going on and a lot of horrifying intimidation. Every one of us was glued to our seats in abject fear, knowing that our turn was coming.

At the break, the student immediately escaped to the bathroom. As a group we were all assembled in the hallway whispering as the assailed student exited the bathroom ten minutes later. The column of students parted as if to allow a royal personage to pass through. The man was pale and weak, being held up by two of his buddies. He had obviously lost his dinner. We never saw him again.

I learned from watching other worms try to wriggle off the hook that the best strategy was to not fight but to let oneself be eaten in one inglorious bite. I learned to accept the humility of preparing for a week and knowing nothing. I learned never to let the professor think I knew anything beyond what he was teaching. I learned that I needed to think totally inside the box. I must never step out of the box created by that professor. First year law school was not the place to know anything. We were in a foreign county that was hostile to our presence. We were learning a foreign language and there would be no deviations. I answered the questions thrown at me with as little animation and embellishment as possible. If he wanted to argue, I stayed as close to the language he was using as I could. I was no fun. He wanted to find students who thought they knew something. Our brainwashing had begun. We were an elite group where total submission to the law was required.

That story is not unlike the life the enemy wants you and me to live. The enemy is a legalist. When we unwittingly make contracts or agreements with him, he holds us to them and will not, no not ever, allow us to wriggle out of it. And he uses fraud, intimidation and deceit. Thankfully, there are *remedies* available in the law and in life with Christ. A remedy is a way of bringing the parties back to wholeness. In our case, while we can be brought to wholeness, the enemy cannot. He made his choice and will live with the consequences for eternity. But that does not mean he will not try to take as many of the human race as possible with him.

In law school I took a whole year to study Remedies. Every area of law has several ways to break off an agreement, to get justice, to get free from an unsavory relationship, to get back to the way it was before the agreement was made. In other words, in the law, it was sometimes called equity or *"to be made whole."*

Contracts can be either unilateral (one-sided) or bi-lateral (both parties must commit to do something in order to form a contract). A unilateral contract is one in which only one party makes a promise or undertakes a performance without first getting the other party to agree. Offers of a reward are generally unilateral. The contract is formed and the reward is owed when you find *Fluffy* and return him to the owner. Nothing is required of you. You could try to find Fluffy or not. There is no obligation on your part. A Biblical example would be the Abrahamic Covenant, explained in Genesis 15, where God is the sole party forming the contract. Abraham did nothing to get what God said He would give him.

A bilateral contract, on the other hand, requires that both parties exchange a mutual promise or agreement. A sale of goods is an example of a bilateral contract. I the buyer agree to pay money and purchase a refrigerator and you the seller agree to sell it to me and promise that it does what refrigerators are supposed to do. A defective refrigerator might be grounds to void the contract.[43]

I have studied and experienced the effects of both law and grace. Grace is better. Because I understand the basics of how a contract works, once I began to see, I was able to understand more clearly the state of my own soul and how I have unwittingly entered into agreements or contracts with the enemy through my brokenness.

Making Agreements with the Enemy

So, how do we make contracts or agreements with the enemy? All territory taken by the enemy of our souls is taken by agreement or some type of permission granted. There are several ways the enemy gains access (permission) to our souls. I mention seven:

1) As we have already discussed, the enemy attaches to the soul through our un-dealt with sin and the garbage it creates. Our sinful attitudes become habits, and manifest themselves as negative thinking in actions and words. Unconfessed sins (words, attitudes, actions) give him permission.

2) Agreements are made through others' sins toward us that touch us in some way, particularly when we are young and vulnerable. Consider sexual abuse, generational cult worship, physical, emotional or mental abuse. Also, consider hurtful words of others toward us. *"I wish you had never been born. We never wanted you. You have ruined my life. You are stupid. You are not pretty. You are..."* These words steal our birthright. God has told us, *"You are my beloved. You are loved by Me."* By believing others' words rather than God's words about us, agreements can be made. Also, when someone hurts us or someone we love we often entertain anger, resentment and a desire for revenge. While we may think this is a natural response, if we hang on to these sins, they can take root and turn into bitterness and/or depression. If we fail to let go of it in the God-prescribed manner, the enemy can gain a foothold.

3) Our own involvement or curiosity about the occult can open a door.

4) Generational curses and bondage that we have already spoken about in Chapter 7 can be an entry point.

5) Our own spiritual weakness and lethargy can create an opening. When we languish on the sidelines of the Christian life and do not seek deeper relationship with Jesus, we can open a fissure for the enemy.

6) When we fail to pay attention to the inner turmoil in our souls or when we fail to listen to the whisper of God's Spirit as He points us toward things, we can generate an opportunity for the enemy as we saw in the John 5 story.

7) We often make vows in our hearts and mind and the enemy tries to force us to keep them. *"I will never be like my mother, I will never allow anyone to hurt me again; No one will ever take advantage of me."* We think they are healthy vows, but beware, all vows can become curses.

While I knew that things happening in my life had a great impact on my way of thinking, I was not aware that I was creating silent strongholds and fortresses around slighting comments I heard as a child, or teasing by kids I didn't know and didn't care about. From people's demands and actions toward me that I felt helpless to control, I built seemingly impenetrable walls. Silent walls were going up as I vowed in my mind that,

> *"I will never let people take advantage of me again. It does not matter if no one likes me. I know I am not pretty, in fact I'm not only not pretty, I am homely so I will work on my personality instead (that sounds noble). Life should be fair. I do more work, yet he is paid more than me. I couldn't possibly do that job."*

Statements like these and hundreds more lurked in the recesses of my mind -- injuring my soul, holding me back, and keeping me from tasting freedom! These words consisted of vows or word curses on my soul that stayed with me, becoming stronger as they were unwittingly affirmed as I went through life.

In the next chapter, we will explore how God begins a rescue operation to free us from faulty thinking and more. This particular Biblical parable has been one of the most powerful weapons God has given me to understand freedom.

Chapter 17. A Rescue Operation – A Biblical Illustration

"The Spirit of the Lord is upon Me,
Because the Lord has anointed Me
To Preach good tidings to the poor
He has sent Me to heal the brokenhearted,
To proclaim liberty to the captives,
And the opening of the prison to those who are bound;" –
Isaiah 61:1 (NKJV)

"How can I know all the sins lurking in my heart? Cleanse me from these hidden faults." Psalm 19:12 (NLT)

"A Christian is held captive by anything that hinders the abundant and effective Spirit-filled life God planned for him or her." – Beth Moore

How Jesus Rescues

Jesus gave us insight into this whole experience of breaking free from the enemy's grip in Mark Chapter 3 when He was confronted and accused by the scribes of acting on behalf of Satan. In a parable, Jesus asked how Satan can cast out Satan and proceeded to explain the impossibility of it. Let's stop here and read Mark 3:20-27. Pay special attention to verse 27 and read the next paragraphs very carefully.

Now that you have read the parable, let's focus on verse 27. Jesus tells us that, *"No man can enter…"* In the Greek it means that *"no man has the power in his own resources"* to enter into the strong man's house. In other words, it would be impossible for you or me in our own strength to form the purpose or intention to overcome the strong man (Satan).

The next part says that, *"no one can enter into his house and plunder his property"*. To "plunder" means to snatch, seize or take from the enemy what he considers his, gained by some legal right. We go into captivity when we knowingly or not make agreements with the enemy to think as he thinks or act like he acts. We also form agreements when we issue vows or word curses about ourselves or others as described in the last chapter. When we fail to take God at His Word and instead choose our own way of thinking, we create a legal right for the enemy to capture that part of our soul.

What or who do you think is the enemy's "plunder" (his property, his goods, his vessels)? It is pretty clear to me that his property refers to the souls of men and includes those of us who have made legal agreements with him. Part of our soul is captive to the enemy until rescue comes.

The next part of the verse says, *"no one can snatch or seize Satan's goods of plunder unless he first binds the strong man."* The word *bind* means to *"put in bonds, deprive of liberty or place in prison."* It also means to wrap up like a mummy. This is exactly what the enemy has done to his plunder. He has placed us in a prison of his making – a stronghold designed to deprive us of liberty.

Baker's Commentary on the Whole Bible says,

> "Jesus' major mission is to invade the house of Satan and free his prisoners…He is engaged in entering the strong man's house, binding up the strong man, and carrying off his possessions…Jesus is proclaiming that in his ministry the kingdom of God is battling against the kingdom of Satan in spiritual warfare and claiming authority over enemy-occupied space…"[44]

When we recognize our enemy has occupied and made captive areas of our soul and we ask Jesus to rescue us, He does to the enemy what the enemy has done to us. He binds him up, sends him off and deprives him of the freedom to move in that part of our soul needing rescue. We must likewise protect the territory by not inviting him back by our words, actions or attitudes. Instead, invite God's Spirit to fill up the now empty space in your soul.

Beloved, when we give the enemy the right to attach to our souls through our traumas and pain, Jesus is the only One who can enter into that part of the soul where the strong man has built a fortress to rescue us and free us. Jesus is the only One with the power to put our enemy in chains and bind him up. So let's put this verse all together:

> *"No man is able or has the power to enter the strong man's house and rescue himself or anyone else who is imprisoned in the enemy's domain. No matter how much we try or purpose to get free, we are unable to free the souls of men in our own power unless we are able to first imprison the enemy and neutralize him. Because we do not have the power to do any of this on our own, we must look to One who is able, One Whose job description includes freeing the captives and setting prisoners free. Only Jesus has the power and authority to free the souls of men."* – combining Mark 3:27 and Luke 4:18

A Personal Example

Now let me give you an example from my life to show you how this happens. We could take any trauma, any emotion or painful event and apply the same or similar pattern. Let's talk about *fear.* Many of us carry fear as a long-term companion on our journey, even though the Word of God tells us in one form or another to *"fear not".* This command appears in over three hundred and sixty five verses, enough to cover every day of the year.

When I was nineteen, my father had a major heart attack the day after Thanksgiving and, in the process, a large percentage of his heart stopped pumping. I am unclear of all the details, but I remember how close he was to death and how all of our lives changed as a result of his experience. He was forty-six and he was the sole source of income in our family except for me who was making $1.65 an hour as a law office receptionist. He was in the hospital for almost a month (he got out Christmas morning).

My mom took my brother and sisters to live with my uncle who was nearer to the hospital. I was left home alone to continue working. I had never lived alone and we did not live in a good area. I began to fear and fret over being home alone at night. I pictured the worst things happening and began to sleep on the couch by the front door so I would hear if anyone was breaking in. Night after night I remember lying awake wondering how I would keep our family going if my father died. I feared someone breaking in to harm me. I had vision after vision of the horrible things that might happen. I remember, as a relatively new Christian, trying to pray but my fears took over and I gave way.

My father thankfully survived the heart attack and was even able to return to work, but the specter remained. My mother was terrified that my father was going to die and made sure none of us made any waves or in any way caused my father stress. I was unable to move out on my own because my financial support became critical to our continued survival. My father knew none of this. The fear of my father dying, or someone else I loved, became huge in my life. It became a stronghold, which followed me into marriage and parenthood. My mother eventually passed away eleven years before my father.

The enemy took a traumatic event from my life and began to whisper all that could/would happen to me as a result. Because I did not see or understand warfare then, fear made deep inroads into my soul.

When I began the journey toward freedom in 2007, I started learning how to pray differently and how to seek freedom. I was also beginning to apply principles I later learned while writing the Mark study, specifically Mark 3:27. I began to understand how the enemy takes us captive into his stronghold.

When my husband became very sick with heart issues in 2015 requiring immediate surgery during Thanksgiving week, my fears began to surface again. This time, I was somewhat armed and ready, though physically I suffered from the results of stress, and fear again kept me awake at night. But this time, with fervent prayer. I determined to trust God in the journey even though fear was making a big noise in my soul. Friends on the journey who knew and understood how to pray against the enemy came alongside to pray for us.

Breaking Agreements

One morning, as I was praying and repenting over giving in to my fears, I asked God for help. I asked Him to take me back with Him to where fear had taken root. I went right back to those moments after my father's heart attack when I was home alone. With Him, in a mesmerizing Scrooge-like journey, I watched the scenario unfold. Only this time, I could see Jesus in the room. He was with me even then. Had I been able to see with spiritual eyes back then, I would not have been afraid. God asked me two questions:

(1) *"Did anyone break in and hurt you?"* (No.)

(2) *"Did your father and your family survive the crisis?"* (Yes, my father lived to be eighty-three.)

At that moment when I realized the lies I had lived with and what a grip fear had had on me for most of my life, I became angry at the enemy and asked God how to break off fear from controlling my life. I did four things:

1) First, I recognized that the enemy gained specific rights to harass me because I gave in to fear and failed to trust God. I

had to learn how to battle specifically. I repented of not trusting God in those moments and allowing fear to gain a stronghold in my soul.

2) I took the authority that I have as a believer in Jesus. In Jesus' Name and His authority I commanded fear to leave and never return. (Review Mark 16:15-18 for the basis of our authority as believers.) I prayed a simple prayer, something like this:

> *"Fear, in the Name of Jesus Christ, I am breaking off any agreement I ever had with you. I take authority over you and command you in His Name to leave. I am covered with the blood of Christ and am in a covenant relationship with Him. His blood covers me and you have no power over me now or ever again."*

3) I then thanked Jesus for His cover, authority and power and claimed victory in His Name by faith. I also asked God's Spirit to take up residence in the areas of my soul vacated by fear. I refused to entertain fear in any way. I was also watchful of its reappearance. When it came upon me, as it has done time and again since that prayer, I stayed in faith and staked a claim on the promise to "fear not" and the promise of my own authority in Christ. I immediately reminded *fear* that its legal right had been broken by the power of Christ in me, His victory on the Cross and His blood shed for me.

4) I began to consciously and deliberately claim the promises in Scripture. I read all the promises relating to fear and began to make them my own. I began to forge them into my mind and insist that my mind not entertain fear, thus learning how to, "take every thought captive."

Was this deliverance achieved in my own strength? No way! I would have been no more than a flea on an elephant trying to assert my way. But with Christ and His authority, the tables are turned. I am now the elephant and the enemy the flea. Do you see the difference?

I am not giving you a formula that will "work every time." As the Spirit grows stronger in your soul, He will speak to you concerning how He wants you to deal with these issues. The point is He wants to teach you war strategies. He desires to grow you up and make you more aware of His Presence. As you follow, He will open your heart and mind to hear more of His mysterious ways and will help you develop your own war strategy.

But the one truth you need to take here is the fact of your authority as a believer. Jesus' own words confirm that He will give us His authority (Luke 9:1) and we must stand firmly upon that and not cringe or falter when the enemy strikes.

In some cases some of you will need more help, counsel and assistance than this book provides. I encourage you not to give up hope but ask God to show you your next step in this area in order to move out and get the help and counsel needed. Consider a Spiritual Director (different from a counselor or psychologist) to help you walk through this journey. Spiritual Directors are often more attuned to the spiritual atmosphere and the places in the soul that need healing. Or you may need to go for prayer to those who are trained in spiritual warfare. Perhaps a Christian counselor or psychologist is what you need to help you, or even a believer gifted in Deliverance prayer. Let Him speak into your soul about His direction and plans.

You may need to do these things and more. There are areas in my life that I need to do more work and get more help. I have gone for counsel and deeper prayer to others who understand the journey of the soul better than I do. I mentioned Dr. Kraft earlier. His books may help and there are many others by other authors who understand this journey.

The importance of the state of our souls and the efforts of the enemy to sneak in require that we understand our own authority in Christ. Let's move on to Part Two of this book, which will help us understand these concepts and describe the many weapons of war in our arsenal. These weapons are powerful to bring down strongholds and were bought for us with the blood of Christ. It is time to wade deeper in for more healing and victory!

PART TWO: STEPPING IN –
REMEDIES AND WAR STRATEGIES

"For though we walk in the flesh, we do not war according to the flesh, for the weapons of our warfare are not of the flesh, but divinely powerful for the destruction of fortresses. We are destroying speculations and every lofty thing raised up against the knowledge of God, and we are taking every thought captive to the obedience of Christ, and we are ready to punish all disobedience, whenever your obedience is complete." -- 2 Corinthians 10:3-5 (NASB)

Chapter 18. The Power Struggle

"...the Lord stood at my side and gave me strength...And I was delivered from the lion's mouth...the Lord will rescue me from every evil attack..." -- 2 Timothy 4:17-18

"There is a holy war afoot with the powers of darkness..." -- E.K. Simpson and F.F. Bruce[45]

Illustration from Nature

We are all familiar with the caterpillar analogy of transformation where the cocoon brings forth an entirely new and beautiful creation. But I did not know this piece: Four times during its life, the moth inside the cocoon sheds its skin and eats what it has shed because it is rich in protein. What *was* plays a part in what it *will be*.[46] The wise Father wastes nothing in our lives. He can be wholly trusted to use every scrap of pain and sorrow we experience in this life. If we are willing and surrendered, He will draw us ever nearer to His side and replace our lies with His truth, planted in us before the foundation of the world.

Transformation was illustrated for us in Jesus' transfiguration (Matthew 17:1-3). The same word is used in Romans 12:1-2. Jesus' nature did not change. He was still fully God and fully man but the disciples with Him were able to see His true God-ness. They could see Who He really is. It is also true for our journey. By following in His footsteps we become outwardly (in our walk) what we are becoming in the depth of our souls. Beloved, God uses everything in our past to bring us to our present and compel us into our future.

Along the same lines, God *gives* us everything we need for transformation -- to stand firm and enter the fray with Him at our side. Every weapon of war we use to go to battle with Him is available to us as we continue to seek a deeper walk. As we walk into Part Two of this book, *Stepping In,* we will look at some of these weapons, many of which you know already and some you might not have thought of. There are more. This book merely taps the surface of battle strategies for believers. Consider it "Spiritual Warfare Strategies 101."

Part of our strategy is to let the enemy know we come from a position of strength. We are more able to resist his cunning when understanding our position. Positionally we are "far above" principalities. (Ephesians 2:4-6) When we armor up, we let the enemy know where we are coming from. As we seek, with God's help, to understand the weapons and authority we have at our disposal, *"weapons to destroy fortresses, speculations and every lofty thing",* we will learn how to stand firm and unmovable in God's mighty care. The Ephesian passage is a good place to start.

The Armor of God

Let's start by reading Ephesians 6:10-21. Make a list of every weapon mentioned. Even if you already know this well, take what knowledge you already have and combine it with what we will be talking about below. Also think about it from the context of war in the soul and getting freedom. I realize that this section of Scripture has many applications covering many areas of life, but I would like you to consider your own life from the standpoint of winning back territory in the continent of your soul.

Scholars generally recognize that Paul used the Roman soldier as his model for describing the armor. He was in prison during the writing of *Ephesians* and was no doubt chained to a Roman soldier. Even though it is unlikely that soldier was fully armed while guarding Paul, other cohorts of the soldier were likely to have been around the prison, thus affording Paul an opportunity to study the various weapons. But he also speaks of the hand-to-hand combat of the

132

Greek wrestler in verse 12. That is because both types of warfare are needed at times.

How to Begin (Ephesians 6:10-11)

When we put our faith in Christ, we receive the armor but we have to learn how to put it on, use it, and trust Christ for the victory. The preliminary comments of Paul leading up to putting on the armor are stated in Ephesians 6:10-11. They are so important to our understanding of this topic. Without these two principles the armor will not help us at all. One without the other is useless. First, in verse ten we are called to be *strong in Him and in the power of HIS might.* I have studied every word of verse 10 and this is what it means:

> *"Be vigorous and strengthened because you are surrounded by and enveloped by Jesus Christ. It is He who is clothing you with His strength. He is in you and He is giving you His authority, His power and the ability and capacity to do whatever is needed to get the job done."*

Start from a place of strength is what Paul advises. This is who you are. You have His authority and power to do what He calls you to do. Ephesians 2:4-6 explains our position, that we are seated with Christ in the heavenlies far above all of the rulers, powers and principalities. Once you understand your position, you will have a better perspective.

Secondly, in verse 11 we are told to put on the armor so we will be able to be stand firm and hold our position, alert and aware of the schemes of the enemy. This is how I read it:

> *"Mentally put on all of the armor every day. You will need every piece every day so you will be able to hold your position and stand unmovable. Putting on all of the armor every day will help you exercise the power you already have been given to endure, persist, stand against and not flee from evil that pursues*

you. Put it on so you will have confidence in your mind and will that the deceit, trickery, craftiness, and ways of the devil will not pull you down, take you out or rob you of what God has for you."

This is what it means to be strengthened with His power and His might and this is what it means to stand firm against the enemy. Make sure you understand your position in Christ and that this is your identity in Christ and why you need the armor. Warfare is only done through Him and the power of His might. Do not even think of trying to fight the enemy in your own strength and power. You *will* fail. Claim these words as your own, make them a part of your story, and learn to help others do the same.

Some of you may be thinking now, *"I don't think I want to do this. It scares me and I am not strong enough the face these kinds of issues."* I know. I have been there and am still there often. But read this graphic story as an example of what happens when you decide not to armor up:

Our pastor, Mike Reed, told a story recently of two rookie policemen in training at the academy. On the last day of training, unbeknownst to them, a demo was set up. A loud gunshot was heard and they all saw the man who shot the gun as the man who was shot fell. After several moments of stunned silence, the man who was shot stood up and bared his chest, showing a bulletproof vest. *"Wear it."* was all he said. They had all the proof they needed. Several months later two of the rookies were involved in a shoot-out with some gang members in Los Angeles. Both were shot. One had a vest on and one did not. The vest that saved the one is on display at the police station today. Both policemen believed in the power of the vest to save them, but only one relied on, put his faith in and depended on the vest to actually do its job.[47] It is a powerful story about how our faith in Jesus saves us, but it is also a powerful story about warfare and the power of God's armor to protect you.

We are either fighting for our own soul freedom (as this book explores) or, through prayer, for the souls of those caught in the enemy's trap. You know by now who the enemy is and that he will stop at nothing to *kill, steal and destroy.* You also know that he is a formidable enemy with an army of destroyers at his service and an arsenal of weapons designed to stop you from doing what you are called to do.

But we are not without resources of our own, divine resources to more than conquer. Take the words of Paul from Ephesians 6:10 and 11. Wear them, learn them, memorize them, teach them and make them your own. Understand who you are in Christ and what He does in you: He envelops you, lives in you, stays with you in battle, and never leaves you. Shore up your understanding of who you are and Whose you are. Understand your position and authority in Him: That He has given you *every weapon* you need to conquer any territory He assigns. **Read. The. Word.**

Whom We are Fighting (Ephesians 6:12-13)

In Ephesians 6:12 Paul defines our "struggle" as a wrestling match, one which involves hand-to-hand combat. It is actually an old word that speaks of one person hurling the other to the ground and holding him or her down with his or her foot on the neck of the loser. It speaks of individual battles and battles requiring speed and deftness. The word is often used of soldiers or athletes.

In Greek wrestling matches the losing warrior had his eyes gouged out resulting in blindness for the rest of his life.[48] Beloved, either you are going to step into Christ and hurl the enemy to the ground, or the enemy will do it to you. You will be knocked out of your ministry, your calling, your purpose, and may live a life of joyless apathy. Finally, you will be blind to his doings in your life. You will miss his attacks and wonder why you are so powerless. We have to learn to fight. Believe me -- I do not want to do it either. But, let's link arms and move out!

Let's stop here and evaluate who Paul is speaking to in these verses. We already know that our struggles are not against flesh and blood, though it may look like it is sometimes (read Ephesians 6:12). Knowing who you are fighting frees you up to love your human enemies because the real enemy is not the human person but the evil being behind and in the person. Forgiveness comes so much quicker because we gain a different perspective, even when someone treats us horribly. Stop here and define in your own words who our struggle is against.

We already know the leader of the evil army is the Devil or Satan. He is the one who:

- Mixes truth with error (Genesis 3:4-5).
- Misquotes Scripture to confuse us (Matthew 4:6).
- Causes false prophets to arise and mimic true believers (2 Corinthians 11:13).
- Binds people's spirits to keep them from doing what God has assigned. (Acts 20:22).
- Enters places he is not expected (Matthew 24:15, 2 Thessalonians 2:4).
- Promises that good can be obtained by wrongdoing (Luke 4:6-7).
- Takes advantage of our pain, suffering and weakness to make forays into the soul, wreak havoc, and takes us captive (Mark 3:27).
- Builds fortresses and strongholds in sacred places and blinds his captives to the truth of it (2 Corinthians 10:3-5).
- Is a murderer from the beginning with no truth in him. (as Jesus described him):

  "Whenever he speaks is a lie, he speaks from his own nature; for he is a liar and the father of lies." -- John 8:44

He is much more than that, but I am not planning to waste any more paper on him. His army of helpers, as we learn here and in other places in Scripture, consist of principalities, rulers, powers, spirit forces of evil (demons) and world forces. Their sole purpose is to keep people out of God's reach or, failing that, make them useless for God's purposes.

The Greek translation for verse Ephesians 6:12 reads,

> *"For we wrestle not against flesh and blood, but against principalities, against powers, against the rulers of the darkness of the world, against spiritual wickedness in high places."*[49]

Paul lists the following antagonists:

- *Principalities* are the premiere leaders of Satan's army. Wuest says they are, "first ones, preeminent ones, leaders."[50] They provide the directives to lower powers.

- *Powers* are the demons who operate in the lower atmosphere. They exercise *exousia* power against people. In other words, power gained by right. They exert power over people and things where they have gained the right to enter through sin, trauma or other woundedness, as we have already discussed in Chapter 16-17.

- *Rulers of the darkness of this world* are Satan and his army who gained legal power and dominion (but not all power) over the earth when Adam sinned. They are the evil spirits who are rulers of spiritual darkness, keeping people in darkness, blinded to the truth, believing error is truth, and unaware that demons even exist. They exert a vicious and malevolent hold over people's minds.

- *Spiritual wickedness in high places* refers to evil rulers who hold "things spiritual" from being seen, understood or known by people.

Beloved, this is why we must war against these powers in God's power, not ours. They exert a strong pull over people to keep them from the truth! God chooses to use people like you and me to bring truth to His beloved humanity. But unless we war to see truth in our own lives, we will not understand why people are so blind to the Gospel. Ignorance of these truths creates a fertile soul for the enemy in battle. A Christian who does not understand his or her covering, his or her righteousness, or the importance of his or her faith can be worn out and become fearful of the adversary. To avoid fear and defeat, we must know how to stand in the armor!

Daniel's Delayed Answer

Remember that even Daniel's answers to prayers were delayed. In Daniel 10:1-14 Daniel prayed and it took three weeks for his answer to arrive, even though God sent the answer on the first day. Verses 12 and 13 explain that the *"prince of the kingdom of Persia was withstanding me for twenty one days…"* It was not until the Angel Michael came to the aid of the delivering angel that the answer was free to be delivered. Like Daniel, we are all caught up in the cosmic war, a collision of kingdoms. We will be either part of the problem or part of the solution. I know whose side I'm choosing!

In the next chapter we will explore the actual armor pieces.

Chapter 19. Armor Up, We're Going In

"The God who girds me with strength...trains my hands for battle." -- Psalm 18:32, 34

"When a man is clothed in righteousness, he is impregnable." --William Barclay

The Armor of God (Ephesians 6:13-17)

Let's look at the armor and plan to don each piece of armor daily in the same order.

The Belt of Truth

Paul says to take up the *full armor* of God. The first piece of armor to put on is the *belt of truth*. The belt had the capacity to hold a lot of equipment and weaponry. It had loops for different knives and swords, depending on the battle; it had loops and compartments for ropes and rations. When those were empty, the soldiers filled them with the spoils of war such as gold and jewels. The belt held everything in place and was tied on to the soldier in several ways so no matter how the soldier moved, when applied properly, the belt was always in place with weapons at the ready. It never got in the way of his movement.

The belt is wrapped around the waist for strength. It also displays strength. The belt was always first to go on in a soldier's armor because nothing else could be attached to the body without it. Think about this in relation to *truth*. When you know the truth and can pull out the principles at any given moment, during any type of battle, you could safely say your belt was on correctly. But if you didn't know the truth, the belt would slide around creating opportunities for the enemy to sneak in. It would slow down the soldier. You would not know how to use the weapons or even be able to readily grab them in the heat of battle. Nor will you be able to spot the enemy twisting the belt, filling your mind with half-truths and errors. You must learn how to apply the Word of God to every situation. *Knowing* the truth is what sets you free. A believer without the truth cannot properly fight the enemy. Start right now. Right where you are spiritually. Take what you know now and begin to apply it and continue to grow and learn more every day. **Read. The. Word.**

The Breastplate of Righteousness (2 Corinthians 5:21)

The breastplate was made of metal plate and chains. It covered the body from the neck to the thighs, front and back. Think about the major organs in our body that the breastplate protects, the heart being foremost. In a Roman soldier, the breastplate was anchored to the belt with rings. Our righteousness is anchored to the belt of truth. We must know the truth of our standing in Him.

Righteousness is our standing with God. It is what Christ gave to us at the Cross. He exchanged His righteous life for my filthy rags. It is only obtained through faith in Christ. It is not something you ask for. It is something you receive on the day you accept Christ. The only problem is, we do not understand Whose we are or who we are in Him. We are already righteous. To put on the breastplate means to acknowledge who you are in Him. Let the enemy know,

> *"I am a child of the King. You have no power over me. I am righteous because of Christ. Do you see my breastplate, which protects my heart and every vital organ? You have no access here. Get out!"*

The breastplate of righteousness is also a weapon of defense against the enemy's accusations and outrageous strategies. He will always aim for the heart because that is where we are prone to fall (Matthew 26:41). But we stand on His righteousness alone! To do anything but that is to fail. **Receive. The. Word.**

The Shoes of Peace

Roman soldiers wore sandals. Some historians credit Roman sandals (and very similar Greek sandals) for their many victories. The footwear were sandals strapped to the ankle and the leg with leather straps, which were difficult to remove. The soles were fitted with spikes to give the soldier a better grounding and a superior posture in battle on hills and poor terrain. The spikes helped soldiers to hold firm in their position.

When your feet are properly shod, you are able to stand firmly on any ground in any battle and maintain your position with confidence. Having God's peace will help you stand firmly planted on the Word of God. You will be able to stay in that place, unmoved by the enemy's lies and threats. Along with the truth, it will protect you when you walk through rough places, places of desolation and despair, places of darkness and dryness. Putting on the peace of God will help you walk anywhere into any situation and it will keep your enemy where he belongs – under your feet! **Wear. The. Word.**

The Shield of Faith

Another word for shield in Greek is "door" or "stone." It referred to a stone for closing the entrance to a cave. It was very heavy and very effective. In later Greek it became known as a large shield used in battle. Its purpose was to extinguish weapons, including fiery arrows and missiles dipped in tar and set on fire before discharge. It was in the shape of an oblong, shaped door and covered a soldier's whole body. He could kneel behind it during an arrow barrage. Though it was large and bulky, soldiers received extensive training designed to give the soldier strength and flexibility when using the shield. Groups of soldiers under siege could form a tight circle and hold shields over their heads to protect them from fiery arrows. Prior to battle, soldiers would soak their wooden shields in water. The shields were covered in layers of leather, so in battle some of the fiery darts would be extinguished by the wet wood and leather. That is why we too must *soak* in the Word of God. If you go to battle with a dry shield, you may go up in flames. Soak your shield in the Living Water!

The shield of faith is an important weapon because the accuser seeks to inject the fiery darts of lies and temptations, doubt, discouragement, unbelief and more into our souls. Things like pride, discontentment, ambition and greed are also difficult to extinguish and continue to smolder and burn within if not dealt with. That is one reason we get faith training every day of our lives. We must learn to use our growing faith as a weapon against the enemy.

What arrows you receive will depend on the weaknesses in your armor (your faith). Evaluate your weaknesses. What causes you the most challenge to your faith? Consider tribulations, fear, anger, persecution, famine, doubt, lust, greed, unbelief, vanity, envy, infirmity, to name a few. Purpose to be ready for any of these challenges. Shore up weaknesses with promises. Get a strategy for each weakness. For example:

- For immorality and lust, flee (1 Corinthians 6:18).
- For unbelief and doubt, speak and quote Scripture and re-focus on Christ (Isaiah 54:17).
- For lack of trust, seize the "Rope of hope" (Romans 15:13).

Paul uses the shield as an example of how to fight using your faith. It is indeed your faith in Him, your faith in the promises of the Word, your faith in who you are in Him that allows you to keep standing in the power life. This is the weapon that extinguishes the fiery darts of the enemy. Let's stop here and evaluate. What weaknesses are in your armor? What areas do you need to pray over to shore up? Note them in your journal. **Believe. The. Word.**

The Helmet of Salvation

The Romans had the best helmet in the ancient world. While other nations used cloth wrappings, animal hides or even bones, the Roman helmet had a chinstrap and visor. Made of bronze (for soldiers) or iron alloy (for officers), it came down to cover the back and sides of the neck. Think today's crash helmets! The helmets had a lining of leather in the inside, softened for comfort and fit. It protected the soldiers from various angles of attack.

The helmet covers the head – the mind. The greatest battlefield the enemy fights over is our mind. The most likely attacks of the enemy will take place in this part of the soul (heart). He wants to undermine our faith, attack our assurance of salvation, create negative thinking patterns, build bad habits, lead us into doubt and much more. It is critical that we understand our salvation – as explained in Chapter Two. We know we are saved eternally. We are righteous because of Christ. Our sins were taken care of at the Cross; our salvation is for our whole journey and includes rescue, deliverance, healing and wholeness of mind, body and spirit at all times. This is what Christ died for.

The enemy is very subtle in these areas. Eve's first mistake was to listen to the enemy. When we listen to the enemy, we are empowering him because our listening gives value to his words. That is why we must listen to God's words revealed through the Scriptures. I have said it before and I am saying it again: take God at His word. The enemy has not only blinded the world but believers as well. We must be alert to his stalking and be ready with the Word of God and prayer.

A note of caution: Even if your head is covered, there may another way the enemy can get into your mind. Consider your eyes, ears and mouth. They are not covered by the helmet. These are gateways to get inside the mind. Take note of what you watch, what you listen to and what you say, and be careful to guard these areas.

Also, beware of walking by sight and not by faith. We cannot be led by our senses alone because everything that is observable to us may not be real truth. As we have already learned, the enemy is a master deceiver and will use any means necessary to pull you down from your calling. One of his main objectives is to get believers to believe that they can lose their salvation. While he cannot steal your eternity, he can render you useless, pull you out and leave you on the sidelines. **Know. The. Word.**

We are going to finish up the last two areas of the armor in the next chapter as we continue to gather up strategies for war. But I want to leave you with this amazing thought. We do not fight *for* victory. We fight *from* victory!

Chapter 20. The Killing Sword

"For the word of God is alive and powerful. It is sharper than the sharpest two-edged sword, cutting between soul and spirit, between joint and marrow. It exposes our innermost thoughts and desires." -- Hebrews 4:12 (NLT)

"God is growing us up in the midst of war...We are allies with Him in the invasion of His kingdom." –John Eldridge

Movie Illustration

In the movie *Saving Private Ryan*, Corporal Timothy E. Upham (played by Jeremy Davis) was recruited by Captain Miller (Tom Hanks) to be the platoon's interpreter after theirs was killed in a particularly violent battle. Miller found Corporal Upham working in the press box safely behind enemy lines. Upham agreed to join the platoon. He admitted to having been trained to use a weapon, but never saw actual combat. As the movie progresses, it is clear that he is not comfortable using weapons and made several choices to do nothing rather than risk involvement. He was dismissively relegated to holding and passing out the platoon's ammunition.

Reading several blogs, I was surprised by how much other soldiers (real ones) disdain having a Corporal Upham in their platoons. Their anger stems from having a brother in the band who is untrustworthy or unreliable in battle. These men and women understand well the phrase, *"I've got your back!"*

In a particularly telling scene, one of the platoon's snipers was trapped in an upstairs room, out of ammo. When Upham rushed up the stairs to provide the ammo, he discovered that an extremely brutal German soldier has gotten there before him. He heard the struggle from outside the door and listened as the German overpowered Upham's comrade using hand-to-hand combat. Upham was frozen with fear and sat on the steps in a stupor of terror unable to move to rescue his dying comrade. After the German killed his prey, he marched out, saw the terrified Upham and indifferently passed him by, not even taking the time to waste a bullet or a bayonet stab:

> *You're no threat; you are already finished; you're on the sidelines; I'm not wasting a second on you; I'm looking for those who know how to fight.*

Such is the situation when the enemy is pressing hard on our souls, using his own particularly violent methods of pulling us down. When we are in a battle for our lives, we had better hope to be surrounded by comrades who have our back. We have all seen the scenarios in movies where the enemy is all over the battlefield. The band of brothers, many of whom are weapons' experts, form a circle and fight from strength to save the day. That's what I want when I'm down: people who know how to pray and use the Word and other weapons to cover me in this war with the enemy.

Fourteen people made a solid commitment to pray for my family and me while I write this book as well as many others who also prayed at specific times for specific situations. These people are my lifeline. When I think I cannot get one more word written, I think of them. Truly, without their commitment to pray, I could not succeed. They believe this book needs to be written and they believe I am the person God has tasked to write it. I am humbled and grateful that God Himself chose these people to walk this part of the journey with us. Thank you. You know who you are!

The Sword of the Spirit Which is the Word of God

As we continue from the last chapter in our study of the Armor of God, we come upon the last item of the armor mentioned:

> *"And take the…sword of the Spirit, which is the Word of God."*

Soldiers carried different types of swords in their belts depending upon the type of battle. The sword that is spoken of here comes from the Greek word *machaira*. This sword was a murder weapon which struck fear into the hearts of those who faced it. A close-encounter type of sword, it was a double-edged, dagger-type sword, which inflicted a wound far worse than any other sword available at that time. The one bearing the *machaira* carried the power of life and death with them. It never brought peace to the enemy. It was a signal of war.[51] It inflicted the most possible damage on its enemies. Only a penetration depth of two to three inches and one twist of the dagger was all that was needed to inflict a mortal wound.

Why would this type of weapon be used to describe the Word of God? Because it is a close-encounter weapon and when we are under attack by the enemy, each word from the Scripture spoken is like a blow to the enemy's head (remember Genesis 3:15). When quoted with authority and consistently when under temptation, the enemy will flee. Learn to use it decisively, not timidly. Quote with confidence, never wavering in the face of the enemy's rage. We saw in Luke 4:13 that that when the enemy *"had finished every temptation"* against Jesus, the enemy left him, *"until an opportune time"* (NASB). God has given us authority to use His words. There is power in the words of God timely delivered. I don't know about you, but I find great satisfaction in picturing the enemy limping as far away from me as possible when I have used the Sword of the Word.

And I want you to see this piece: Who does the sword belong to? Scripture says it belongs to the Spirit. A work of the Spirit is to call to remembrance every verse we study when needed. He is the One who frees up the soul to make room for more of His presence. It is the sword of the Spirit entrusted to us by the Spirit. **Use. The. Word.**

In Chapter 10 we talked about how Jesus protected His birthright. He used the Sword of the Word with great power. One of my closest friends, Linda MacCubbin calls it the "greatest sword fight ever". And she reminded me of this piece:

> *"Satan also knows the Word so we must be doubly careful in developing our listening skills for the still, small voice. We must be so attuned to true truth that when the enemy with subtlety twists the truth, we can discern the distinctions. If the enemy can get you to doubt the truth, you do not have a weapon to fight him."*

Thanks, Linda!

How God Gives Us the Right Words to Use
In a 1991 study a cardiologist discovered that,

> *"The heart has an elaborate circuitry that allows it to act independently of the cranial brain in its ability to learn, remember, sense and feel."* [52]

According to recent science, our bodies contain two brains, the *heart* brain and the *mind* brain. When you hear a truth or read it in Scripture, it begins to work its way from the *mind* brain to the heart. But sometimes the message does not get delivered to the heart (often, I would say). It gets sidetracked, robbed or stolen from us by the enemy. He uses our own thinking to cinch the crime. What happens is that when some truth you have heard or read begins to work its way to your heart, it can be suddenly expelled because of unbelief, some fear, past experience or even inattention. We can train our minds to receive, which we will cover in a later chapter. But so often the word gets snatched from us before it can take root in the heart. (See Mark 4.)

We need God to heal our broken hearts or the way our broken hearts think. From our head to our heart, we are just inches away from victory! As we get more healing in our soul (heart), we are able to intake and keep the Word hidden there to be used for situations like enemy encounters. The Spirit, as the holder of the sword (Word) inserts the promises into our lives at just the right moment. It's the *I read this passage a thousand times and never saw it until this moment* syndrome. He implants the promises and gives direction and encouragement at just the right moment. There are many ways to get the Word into your heart as in the following:

- Memorizing: Hiding His Word in your heart is exactly like storing up supplies for a rainy day or a future crisis.
- Meditating: Focusing on a verse, a part of a verse (or even a word), to listen to what God is saying to you.
- Reading the Bible chronologically. (I use the Chronological Bible for my devotional time, reading a small section from the Old Testament, the gospels and Psalms every day.)
- Looking up root word meanings by researching the true meanings of the words and applying them to your situation (as we have done in this book).

Beloved, whatever way you can get the Word into your head and into your heart, go for it. I am sure many of you have strategies that work for you. Make a note of those in your journal or notebook because you never know when you might be called upon to assist another with that weapon.

The Bible tells us it is a *Living Word*. (Hebrews 4:12) That means it speaks to every generation right where they are. It speaks to every individual soul as the Spirit looks over your shoulder and points out verses you may have read a thousand times but never really saw. You know my story, that I was completely changed by reading *the whole verse* of John 10:10, not just the abundant life part. Everything crystallized for me when I understood why I was not living the abundant life and that for years the enemy had been deceiving me, stealing from me, trying to kill and destroy every effort I tried to do with God. That's over! I am on to him in this area and I am learning how to wield that deadly sword, showing no mercy!

So many good books out there give excellent overviews of the Bible or excellent resources for how to glean truth from it. I do not plan to do that here. What I will do is to give you some tips that I have learned over the years in my reading of the Bible. You will develop your own methods as you commit to hiding His Word in your heart. Learn to read the Word with a mind open to what the Spirit is saying. So often we read only to reinforce our current beliefs, with minds set on hearing only what we believe, but to truly see, be willing to open to how He sees.

Read Devotionally

As I indicated earlier, I read the Chronological Bible as my devotional reading in the morning. I do not follow the "One Year" plan. I find that too stressful and limiting. It usually takes me about two years to go through the Bible once. Consider these points:

- Before reaching the end of the current reading cycle, I begin asking in prayer for God's Spirit to place certain words on my heart to look for as I begin the next cycle. Over the years I have watched for, circled and meditated on, verses containing words like, "heart", "soul", "treasure", "hidden", "mystery", "bondage", "idols", "prison", "darkness", "praise", "worship" and many others. These words help me focus on where I am in the journey and where He is working.

- Starting from Genesis I read a small section every day. I also do a short reading from a section of the gospels and a Psalm or part of a Psalm.

- Reading from the Old Testament, I ask the Spirit to nudge me at anything I need to take note of. When that occurs I stop reading there and ask myself, *"Is there some lesson to be observed from the reading that I or someone I know might benefit from?"* *"What is God saying here?"* (For example, I might write a couple verses in my journal accompanied by whatever commentary comes to mind about those verses.).

- Whenever battles are mentioned I take particular note of strategies used. I look to how God responds and speaks, whether or not the battle is done under His cover, whether or not prayer preceded it, whether that made any difference in the outcome, and who prevailed and why? These are important things to know for our own development of spiritual strategies in the heavenly places. The battles and opposition faced by the Israelites in the Old Testament are not there for just historical purposes, but to help us understand for our own lives how to go to war with the enemy of our soul.

- Reading from a section of the gospels, I always want to stay in Jesus' footsteps, following His journey carefully. I make note of His healings, how He heals, what He says, how He teaches and speaks. I look for how He leads, what instruction He gives to His disciples and what the parables might be saying about life and journey. I want to *hear* His voice every day.

- Finally, reading a Psalm or a portion of one every day lets me look for "soul" words and "heart" words so I can learn how the psalm writers thought and lived out their journey. This teaches me how to praise and worship God. I read the psalm to myself, then aloud, as a prayer, often inserting my own name or even someone else's when appropriate. When the psalmist talks about his *enemies* always dogging him and doing evil to him, it's not *people* I see as the evil ones but our enemy Satan and his minions.

Learn to use whatever time you have to build His Word into your life, regularly and consistently so that it sticks with you. David meditated in the night watches (Psalm 42:8); and sometimes in the morning (Psalm 5:1-3). Jesus got up while it was still dark to pray (Mark 1:35). Prayerfully consider what might work with your schedule. Give Him the best part of your day, when you are most alert. Can you get up a few minutes earlier or go to bed a few minutes later? Do you have a break time at work that you could use? Can you listen to the Scriptures and pray on your commute? Think outside the box and ask God's Spirit to help you define a time that might work.

While listening to sermons are also excellent, make sure your priority is *your time* in the Word with God's Spirit teaching you. That is what speaks deeply to your soul. Words of others may help you get the Word in you, but it is your obedience to opening the Word that will help you the most. Do not become dependent on any one preacher or teacher. Learn how to listen to His Spirit and if you cannot *hear*, do not give up.

Reading to Study

My study time in the Word is different from the time I spend in prayer and meditation in the Word. I learned a long time ago not to substitute time in the Throne Room for time preparing to teach or minister. They are *not* the same thing. Time in the Throne Room in prayer and meditating on Scripture is the holy moment of every day where you are cloistered in His Presence. He waits with longing for that time with you, and, soon, you will long for it also. It is where He reveals His mysteries; it is where He speaks to things of your heart and things that concern you; it is where He reveals to heal; it is where He exposes the hidden things that keep you down and hold you back; it is where you leave your burdens; it is where you worship and praise

152

Him. This is a time to BE in His presence without any agenda. It is the Mary time (Luke 10:38-42).

Study time, on the other hand, is the time you spend personally reading and learning the Word. It also may be necessary preparation for leading or participating in a Bible Study class. This study time helps you understand and apply the Scriptural knowledge. You may study words in their original language and historical background or review commentaries or sermons. These all enhance your Biblical understanding and are very important, but they do not substitute for time alone with Him.

Choose a Staff

Benjamin Vaughn Abbott spoke of Psalm 23:4, *"Your rod and staff comfort me."* He explains that when he was a boy his father had a small closet in his country home that contained a variety of walking sticks left over from generations of his family. He reported that often he would go to the closet and choose a staff appropriate for the walk he intended to make. He made a spiritual application that I think is so apt for our own journeys. He applied the various staffs to represent the promises God gives us in His word.[53] For example:

- When discouragement overtakes you, pick up the staff of Psalm 42:11:

    "Why are you in despair, O my soul? And why have you become disturbed within me? Hope in God, for I shall yet praise Him. The help of my countenance, and my God."

    (You might also consider asking yourself the same question asked by the psalmist here. "Why is *my* soul hurting?")

- When loss strikes, pick the staff of Psalm 30:5: *"Weeping may endure for the night, but joy comes in the morning."*

- When illness strikes, choose the staff of Isaiah 30:15: *"In quietness and trust shall be your strength."*

- When you feel under condemnation, pick Romans 8:1: *"There is therefore now no condemnation in Christ Jesus."*

- When the enemy strikes, select Isaiah 54:17: *"No weapon formed against you shall prosper."*

- And, when you are brokenhearted, grab Psalm 34:18:

> *"The Lord is near to the brokenhearted and saves those who are crushed in spirit."*

You get the idea. There are promises for every situation in the Scripture. Go search them out and claim them. Make them a part of your arsenal to use against the enemy when he comes armed with doubt, discouragement and destruction. Do not be taken out!

Chapter 21. The Believer's Umbrella

"You faithfully answer our prayers with awesome deeds, O God our Savior. You are the hope of everyone on earth, even those who sail on distant seas." – Psalm 65:5 (NLT)

"You can do more than pray after you have prayed, but you cannot do more than pray until you have prayed...Prayer is striking the winning blow...service is gathering up the results."
-- S.D. Gordon[54]

Prayer – The Umbrella over All

There are many, many weapons of war in the heavenly arsenal, but the last one expressed in the following Ephesians 6 passage is prayer. It is one of two weapons that covers all (the other being the blood of Christ, discussed in the next chapter).

"And pray in the Spirit on all occasions with all kinds of prayers and requests. With this in mind, be alert and always keep on praying for all the Lord's people. Pray also for me, that whenever I speak, words may be given me so that I will fearlessly make known the mystery of the gospel, for which I am an ambassador in chains. Pray that I may declare it fearlessly, as I should." – Ephesians 6:18-20 (NLT)

My good friend, Linda MacCubbin (my armor expert, who says she learned this concept from Kay Arthur) speaks of prayer being like a walkie-talkie, a two-way communication between you and God. Unfortunately, she expounds, too often we forget to release the button after talking so we can hear what the other side is saying. We fail to listen to the Commander's suggestions. That leaves us in control of the situation, but *He* is the One who has all of the combat intelligence for the particular battle we are about to step into. He is the One who knows which way is clear, what weapons are the most effective, what strategy to employ. When you fail to release the button on your heavenly walkie-talkie, you will become easy prey for the enemy. He will get you to doubt:

> *"He has forgotten you; you are out here all alone; you have waited too long and now you are surrounded; are you sure you want to go that way?"*

Prayer is a two-way communication and, as the old saying goes, "Practice makes perfect." In this case, as you pray more, seeking more room in your soul for Jesus, seeking a closer walk with Him, He delights in making it happen. His Spirit will, *"teach you all things"* (John 14:26).

The main point to understand about prayer is that it is the *umbrella* needed over every soul, every ministry, every undertaking in the spiritual and natural realms. This includes every doctor visit, every parent-teacher visit, every trip, every communication, every illness and every breath taken. It is the gift of community with God and it is His chosen method of communicating with us. Prayer is His vehicle for activating and manifesting the spiritual realms over us.

Pray in the Spirit (Ephesians 6:18)

Prayer increases the power of the armor and prayer itself contains many additional weapons. Very simply stated, prayer can be defined as "talking with God." Note the use of the preposition "with" not "to". I am pretty stuck on prepositions. As a lawyer, I have used prepositions as an amazing tool to help form and win cases. As a former law professor, I taught my students to use prepositions to argue for or against various positions in the law.

In the Ephesians passage (Ephesians 6:18), Paul uses the phrase, "pray *in* the Spirit" (used only twice in the New Testament, the other being Jude 20-21). Another way of describing it is to say that we pray "by means of" the Spirit. In other words, using His thoughts to our mind, under His influence and with His assistance (see also Romans 8:26). And because He is in you, He can pray through you and prompt you to pray His direction. Of course, the more room in your soul there is for Him to operate as discussed in Part One, the more we are able to hear, to speak and to move.

All Kinds of Prayers and Requests

In verse eighteen, Paul tells us to pray, "*On all occasions with all kinds of prayers and requests,*" but in the Spirit (or Spirit-directed). "All kinds of prayers" contains within its boundaries the means of deliverance, wisdom, strength, confession, repentance, forgiveness, professions of faith, adoration, thanksgiving, praise, intercession and more. Like a Swiss army knife, prayer contains a whole horde of other weapons, some of which we will take up in the next chapter. Paul speaks about this in verse eighteen where he says to "*pray with all prayer and supplication.*" Different situations require different types of prayer. Sometimes a prayer of wisdom or strength is needed. Consider these insights:

- Prayer, praise and thanksgiving are powerful atmosphere changers.
- Intercession is a focused, alert, attentive prayer over a specific situation for an extended period of time for a specific outcome. It is a way of getting the mind of Christ over the person or situation we are burdened to pray over.
- Deliverance prayers ask Jesus to enter into the strong man's house and free the captive (Mark 3:27).
- Repentance, confession and cleansing prayers help us clean up the soul to make more room for Him.
- Meditative prayer is the means by which we come into God's presence. It is a way of telling Him, "*You are here and I am here. I want You but how it happens is up to You.*" It is a way of letting

go or surrendering everything but Him and attuning to His heart.

There are many more types of prayer than listed above. Some types of prayer take additional training to learn.

How God Answers Prayer

I want you to be aware of *how* God sometimes answers prayer so you will not be misled or deceived. Sometimes the answers will come one piece at a time. Perhaps you will receive a phone call from a wayward son, rather than a full-blown return. Sometimes pieces of answers will come in dreams or a Scripture verse timely read. At times, someone else's words will provide a piece of the answer. Just as healing is often a process, the same is true of prayer. We need to train ourselves to be alert to whatever He shows us through whatever means and to be expectant that He intends to answer.

Often we expect the whole answer all at once, but if we learn to exercise faith when we receive a small piece, more will come. It is one way God builds our faith. We need to learn to build a miracle tree over our prayers. Whenever a piece is answered, put another leaf on the tree and keep a praise journal.

Such is how Jesus taught His disciples and built their faith. He told them over and over that He would leave them at some point. They had trouble receiving His words, but He kept giving them more pieces as the journey went on. Even though they experienced the death of the vision they had of Messiah's coming after He was crucified, they later remembered what Jesus had told them. His resurrection, while not the answer they believed would come, certainly changed everything. Beloved, do not give up hope. Keep praying with a persistence that speaks of faith in the One who is faithful.

Be Alert and Pray for All God's People (Ephesians 6:18)

When Paul tells his hearers to "be alert with all perseverance", he is warning them to stay awake, be ready, vigilant, not weary, not negligent, not careless. No soldier prays for himself or herself alone. They pray for the whole platoon and for a common cause. Your prayers for a fellow soldier fighting alongside of you may be what saves the day in your own life in a future battle. Some of my friends are prayer intercessors on the front lines in battles for nations and world leaders. That is not my call, but in my small way, I pray for God to strengthen them for the battle He has assigned them and I pray over their own heart concerns. Often I in turn receive their mighty prayers in my own battles. When we pray for one another, we are strengthened in our respective journeys. Praying for fellow soldiers in the battle with you is praying in unity that each one might overcome rather than be overcome. Jesus said,

> *"For where two or three are gathered together in my name, there am I in the midst of them."* -- Matthew 18:20 (KJV)

While He often prayed alone, He also taught His disciples to pray in community. In John 14-16, Jesus prays for the disciples in a way that they can hear, understand and learn. In the garden He asks three of His disciples to pray for Him. In groups He often raised His eyes and hands to heaven to thank God for provision. Learn to pray with and for fellow soldiers in the battle with you. Do not just pray for their everyday needs, but pray for their core to be strengthened; pray for God to raise them up in battle even as He is raising you up. Strong unity is a cord that cannot be broken. Remember, the enemy will do anything and everything to divide, isolate and thus conquer more easily. But you stand firm.

Paul's Example of What to Pray (Ephesians 6:19-20)

Paul asks for prayer for boldness:

> *"Pray also for me, that whenever I open my mouth, words may be given me so that I will fearlessly make known the mystery of the gospel, for which I am ambassador in chains. Pray that I might declare it fearlessly as I should."* -- Ephesians 6:19-20 (NIV)

It is so instructive to see how Paul prays and desires his prayers to be answered. He is in prison, chained to a prison guard, but does not ask to be released; he does not ask to be vindicated; he does not ask to be taken out of his situation; he does not ask for his needs to be met or for more comfortable circumstances (which is probably what I would be praying). Instead, he asks that he be empowered to be *obedient* to the call, that he be courageous in delivering the words he was given by God, and that he might speak fearlessly to those God brings. Do you pray this over your pastor, leaders, friends on the journey? Brothers and sisters, we can learn a lot from this prayer on how to ask for prayer in our own situations! Pray healing? Yes. But also pray to be strengthened, encouraged, and enabled to be outward thinking. Be asking for prayer on how to use your situation to glorify God and bless others.

Some Additional Helps on Prayer

I have been reading books, pouring over the Scripture and learning how to pray for so many years. But what it all boils down to is asking God's Spirit to lead us in our conversations with God:

> *"How should I pray over this? How can You be glorified in this? Is there something I need to know, see or do about the situation I am in? What am I to learn in this situation? Is there something I can do to help this person through their trial? How should I pray for rulers, governments, nations and those in authority?"*

It is learning to ask questions and listen for the holy nudges from His Spirit pointing us in a direction, putting in our minds a task, a thought, a Scripture, a notion of what He wants. I offer the following suggestions on how to make this happen:

- Donna Partow teaches us to pray the solution, not the problem. I am learning not to bemoan the situation I'm in (or someone else is in). I thank God that He already has a plan; that His way is the best way. I thank Him for His wondrous and mighty works. I give Him praise (or I pray a psalm). I recall to Him His characteristics of goodness, love, mercy and grace.

- Keep a "to do" sheet nearby, so when distracting thoughts inevitably come concerning tasks needing to be done, write them down and then refocus on prayer.

- Be specific in your prayers – not general. Faith can't grow by seeking His answers to prayers such as, *"God bless everyone; or God, bless my son."* How will you know when it is answered? In my younger days, I used Stormie O'Martian's books on *The Power of a Praying Parent* and *The Power of a Praying Wife* to assist me. They seemed to cover the areas I was concerned about for my husband and son and they helped me learn how to pray positively and specifically.

- Pray the prayers of the Bible for people and yourself. For example, look at Colossians 1:9-12, Ephesians 1:15-20 and Philippians 1:9-11. As you learn to read the Scriptures with discernment, you will see other prayers that you can incorporate for yourself, your family, friends and other situations.

- Do not just list people, prayers and problems. Ask God's Spirit whom He wants you to pray for, what He wants you to pray, and how He wants you to pray. Look at the list of partial forms of prayer above. Should you pray deliverance, praise over the person, wisdom, strength or in some other manner?

- Be ready to move out and obey what you hear God saying to you. God is action-oriented, always speaking, answering, leading. Do not sit on the sidelines hoarding what God has given to you. Get moving!

- Pray with authority by using His words. *"In Your Word, you state...", "Thank you for the promise of your Word that says...", "Thank You for Your Word which promises..."* You will get no grief from God if you remind Him of His words. You might even consider highlighting various prayers in your Bible to access them easily.

- Praise, praise, praise and worship! We will cover this in a later chapter, but I always begin by thanking God and I end by praising His Name, magnifying His character and showing gratitude for His care over me and those I pray over. Not as a formula, but out of a heart that knows He is in the midst and is concerned about every issue that concerns me.

These few suggestions do not even tap the surface, but my hope and prayer for you is that you will be energized to come in to His presence more. You will find delight, joy, help, strength and more by being with Him. Imagine, being in the Presence of the Creator of the universe! Even more, understand that *He* is the one who longs for community with you! **Pray. The. Word.**

In closing this chapter, when we put on the armor, we are "putting on" Jesus Christ. Understanding not only what Jesus Christ has done for us, but Who He really is reveals that He is a picture of the Armor of God:

162

"...clothe yourselves with the Lord Jesus Christ, and do not think about how to gratify the desires of the sinful nature." – Romans 14:13 (NIV)

- He is our "belt" (the belt holds all of the other pieces together) (Colossians 1:16, John 14:6).
- He is our righteousness (2 Corinthians 5:21, Jeremiah 23:6).
- He is our peace (Ephesians 2:14).
- He is our shield (Galatians 2:20).
- He is our salvation (Luke 2:30).
- He is our sword (Ephesians 6:17).
- He is the Word of God (John 1:1, 14).

I want to close this chapter with a quote by a beloved saint, Oswald Chambers, almost a household name to believers. Of prayer, he says this,

"Thou art the God of the early mornings, the God of the late at nights, the God of the mountain peaks, the God of the sea, but my God, my soul has further horizons than the early mornings, deeper darkness than the nights of the earth, higher peaks than any mountain, greater depths than any sea. Thou who art the God of all these, be my God. I cannot search to the heights or the depths; there are motives I cannot trace and dreams I cannot get at; my God, search me out and explore me and let me know that Thou has done so."[55] *Amen!*

Chapter 22. Receiving and Setting Free

"Bear with each other and forgive one another if any of you has a grievance against someone. Forgive as the Lord forgave you."
-- Colossians 3:13 (NIV)

"Forgiveness is the doorway through which we pass into a new life". – Lawrence O. Richards

Movie Illustration

A number of years ago we saw a movie that was both challenging and moving at the same time. *The Mission* starred Robert DeNiro as a slaver named Mendoza who enslaved natives of South America in the 1700's and sold them to work the plantations.

When Mendoza found his fiancée in a compromising situation with his half-brother, he challenged the man to a duel and killed him. Mendoza received no sentence legally since dueling was not a crime. But he experienced a sentence of his own making instead. Rather than relief from the vengeance he sought, Mendoza experienced a deep depression and mourning over what he had done, confining himself to a cell in a monastery. Mendoza, like many of us, could see no way out of the blackness in his heart.

Months later he was visited by one of the fathers, Father Gabriel (Jeremy Irons) who challenged him to a penance[56] of serving the very people he once sold into slavery. Thus, Mendoza began the journey to the interior bogged down with a bundle containing all of his armor, the breastplate, helmet, and sword. In a way it was a penance for Mendoza to carry the very things that caused harm and death to those he was going to serve. Although I do not believe it is necessary to make penance for our sins in the way Mendoza did, it is the picture of hauling the baggage representing his sin that I want you to see.

As the treacherous trek up the mountains continued, Mendoza became more and more weighed down by his baggage. Because of its weight, he fell, slid down hills, was cut by rocks, and hit trees only to slog back to the path caked in mud, which dried on him making the journey even more miserable. At one point one of the other missionaries on the journey in a fit of pity cut the rope sending the bundle hurtling down the mountain, only to have Mendoza in a crazed haze, climb down to retrieve the bundle and crawl back up the hill with the bundle tied behind.

With Mendoza lagging far behind, the weary travelers finally reached the natives they pledged to serve. When he arrived and the villagers realized he was the one who had sold their families into slavery, there was a lively discussion about whether to kill him or not. One native grabbed a knife and pulled Mendoza, now on his knees from fatigue, by the hair and held the knife to his throat. Mendoza was quietly submissive almost as though he wished to be put out of his misery. A tense few moments were suspended on the screen as everyone waited to see what would happen. Suddenly, the native removed the knife from Mendoza's throat and reached behind him, cutting the bundle from Mendoza's waist. He then pushed Mendoza's past over the side of the cliff until it disappeared. Mendoza was free and so were the natives.

I love this part of the movie because it so vividly pictures what forgiveness looks like and feels like. Forgiveness is a powerful weapon in a believer's arsenal. It changes people – both the giver and the receiver.

There can be no denial that the sins of others against us can brutally affect us and often restoration seems impossible. Regret is too small a word to ever cover the loss. The grit and grief of sin, ours and others' can change the course of our lives in an instant, sending us swirling down a rabbit hole from whence we might never crawl out. But God...!

In my story, which we explored in Part One, I also struggled with forgiveness. I had a single space two sided, two column list of people that at one point I believed had forsaken my friendship. They were people who said they would walk the journey with me, but couldn't. That is just about every friend or family member I have or have ever had. That is a lot of friends who didn't even know they were on my list! I was in a dark place and I was desperate for freedom. I needed to learn that no one could wholly walk through things with you except God. Dependence on Him alone is His will. My unforgiveness created a heavy burden not unlike Mendoza's bundle of armor. It also placed me in a solitary prison of my own making.

I was finally able to ask for and receive God's forgiveness. I then asked the Spirit to go back with me to every person so I could forgive them. I pictured every dear face that I believed had hurt me in some way and, with the Spirit's help, I cut them loose in my mind. Some I could not let go of right away; others were easier. I saw the almost invisible cord that had wrapped around me begin to unravel. I set them free so I was no longer holding on to them.

Beloved, when you do not forgive someone, you are holding them back, tied to you with an invisible cord. Your unforgiveness may be holding them back from God's best for them just as it holds you back from His best for you. They are the prisoner and you are the jailer. Neither of you is free to go on about the business of life.

I did not go back to these people physically for various reasons, but mostly because having to explain what I felt they had done to me (without their knowledge) could have created guilt in them or offended them. In truth, it was my faulty perception more than it was any action of theirs. When I set those beloved people free to move on with their lives, I was suddenly free to move on with mine. It was an exhilarating moment. I was no longer dogged by the perceived failures of others; I could look them in the eye with a deep love, knowing we had all been unchained. In truly understanding God's forgiveness, we are enabled to see others as weak and needy too. Most of these people on my "list" did nothing to get there. I had to learn how to exercise *horizontal* forgiveness even as I experienced *vertical* forgiveness from God. Forgiveness is both vertical (between you and God) and horizontal (between you and others).

Vertical Forgiveness – I Receive God's Forgiveness

Forgiveness, faith and mercy are inexplicably bound. God's mercy operated to forgive us for His Son's sake. Our faith in the completed sacrifice of Christ receives the forgiveness. While creation was accomplished with a word from God's mouth, our forgiveness took the death of His Son. He offers it willingly and you can do nothing to get it except receive it. At the moment of placing your trust in Jesus Christ, it is a finished event! You have been forgiven of all sin, past, present and future. It is part of the salvation journey toward wholeness we spoke about earlier. The capacity to forgive and be forgiven is grown in us as we walk with Him, and the result is that we experience more freedom in our souls and more room for His Spirit to work in us.

The most challenging part about God's forgiveness is the simplicity of receiving it. The Scriptures over and over tell us the deed is done. (See Ephesians 1:7 and 1 Peter 2:24.) But somehow, we cannot receive it. Even the apostle Paul had trouble with the truth of it. Review Romans 7:14 to 8:2 to see how he finally solved the issue in his soul. There are many, many verses in the Bible that *prove* you are forgiven. But unless the truth of the words reaches your heart, you will not be able to receive them, even though you are eternally saved and His Spirit dwells in you. It is something only accomplished through faith (Ephesians 2:8-9). I suggest you meditate on these verses and command your heart to line up to believe it and receive it until it is *finished* in your life and you own this truth!

168

The process of forgiving from the Divine side is incredibly complicated and immeasurably costly, demanding nothing less than the complete satisfaction of God to meet the demands of His outraged holiness. The intricate sacrificial system of Leviticus tells the tale, where every thread of Leviticus leads us to the understanding that in order for forgiveness to happen, blood must be shed. Hebrews 9:22 says,

> *"And according to the Law, one may almost say, all things are cleansed with blood and without the shedding of blood there is no forgiveness."*

The Old Testament counterpart found in Leviticus:

> *"For the life of a creature is in the blood, and I have given it to you to make atonement [forgiveness] for yourselves on the altar; it is the blood that makes atonement for one's life [sins]."* – Leviticus 17:11 (NIV)

It is beyond the scope of this book to explore the concept with you more. I wish we could. It is a story of such horror, beauty and divine love that no one but a Holy God who desperately loves the unlovely and desires their presence in eternity could come up with such a costly way of reconciliation and restoration.

In sum, where sin destroyed the relationship between you and God, it was the Cross that created the bridge to close the gap. The Old Testament explained that the only acceptable sacrifice was the blood of a perfect lamb. The New Testament teaches us that the sacrificial Lamb was none other than God's only Son who willingly went to the Cross. He is the Lamb of God who takes away the sin of the world. (John 1:29) He was the only one who could free us. He was the one who refused death until it could be done in the only acceptable way. He was the one who, near death, willed it away to crawl to the Cross so He could finish the deed. And when He had done so and uttered

His final words, "It is finished", it was done indeed. All sin, past, present and future was nailed to the Cross.

Horizontal Forgiveness – I Forgive You and Me

Forgiveness is a weapon of war that keeps you walking in freedom. C.S. Lewis said,

> *"To be a Christian means to forgive the inexcusable because God has forgiven the inexcusable in you."*

One of the words in the Greek for forgiveness is *aphiemi*. It means, *to forgive, leave, or release from captivity*. It can also mean to send away. So the words have the elements of mercy, freedom from captivity and the concept of sending your sin far away from God *and* from you. When I forgave my list of friends and family, I sent what I perceived they did to me away from me and released them from being held captive to me by the invisible chains. God did the same to me because He had freed me from prison and being chained to an unforgiving enemy who will never dispense one second of grace. God's forgiveness of me completed the deed.

When you refuse to forgive, you are the one caught. You will not be fully released to move on and neither will they. When we keep things alive in our minds, it continues to live on in us and fuels us. As long as it lives in us, we can still be hurt by it – by the stress it causes, by the anxiety we feel when it comes up, by the emotional pain, and by the desire to hurt back. Unforgiveness opens fissures in the soul for the enemy to sneak in. Indeed, there are some who do not deserve our forgiveness, but to withhold it is not living and walking as Jesus did.

A Personal Example

I recently developed an ear fungus from water in my ear. When the doctor gave me antibiotics believing it to be an infection, the fungus grew worse because antibiotics kill bad bacteria *and* good bacteria, thus creating an environment for the fungus to grow unrestrained.

There was nothing left to fight the fungus after the antibiotic did its job. It was allowed to multiply unhindered. It delayed healing and resulted in some hearing loss. Unforgiveness is like that fungus. When unforgiveness is allowed to remain in the soul to fester and grow with nothing to counter-act it, it builds a strong fortress around it which, if not dealt with, can infect our whole life. A root of bitterness can spring up and chances are good that when we harbor unforgiveness, we will not be able to hear God's voice. The fungus of unforgiveness blocks hearing.

One author (I can't currently recall) defined *bitterness* as *unfulfilled revenge*. It can spread like a weed and can eventually cause your own heart to shut down. Yielding to bitterness and refusing to forgive allows the enemy to gain a foothold in you possibly robbing you of your capacity to love. Wishing to protect yourself, you might burrow in, isolate yourself and lose your capacity to look on others with love, not wanting to be hurt again.

I would like you to stop and think about this with spiritual eyes and how my story of the fungus can look in your soul. Is your *immune system* strong? Are you able to ward off the fungus before it takes root by forgiving early on? Or is your soul a welcoming place for darkness to fester? Are you afraid of being hurt? Are you harboring bitterness against someone or someones? Is there someone you cannot let go of? Perhaps your perception of God and His apparent unwillingness or inability to help you in your situation has caused you to become bitter toward Him. Pray on this one and ask for revelation. Ask for forgiveness. It can happen easily and you may not even be aware of it. Now would be a good time to review and think about your journey and ask God to show you those that you need to forgive, including God Himself. Allow the Spirit to speak. And ask Him to expose in you areas in your own soul where you need to ask forgiveness.

You do not, however, need to spend the rest of your life searching out things in the soul if you are on a journey with Him. Trust Him to reveal to heal in the best time. But be sensitive to His leading as He may ask you to forgive areas you normally wouldn't think about. Consider corporations or employees who cheated you or stole from you; doctors who pledged to help you, but instead took the easy way out causing serious life challenges. The wounds and traumas brought on by others can create serious soul wounds that need to be healed. Honestly, some of these things can seem so paltry and small, but like the Veggie Tales *Rumor Weed*, they can grow into giant weeds that block out the sun and cover other hidden weeds. It is not worth the cost of your freedom. The person you need to forgive may not deserve a better life, but you do.

I have been surprised by how much unforgiveness is hidden in my own soul: The hospital whose caregivers let my mother die; the staff of a Christian organization I worked for as a young believer whose actions and hurtful words spoke that I was unwelcome because I was different than they were; even an uncle who teased me unmercifully about being a redhead.

Unforgiveness affects the heart. God wants you to experience abundant living but you cannot when you are still shackled by the enemy's chains. Choose *yes* to forgive, to not hold bitterness. Learn to take every thought captive. When that matter comes up in your mind, take control of it. Here are some things I have worked through and tried to incorporate into my life on this issue:

- Do not let your thoughts wander or go to the, "*I would say this…*" or "*He would say this…*" scenario. Take every thought captive and ask the Holy Spirit to give you a nudge or a check. He tells me, "*Don't go there*" when I threaten to roll into the rabbit hole.
- If necessary, take the initiative, even if you are the one who is wronged (Matthew 18:15-20, Ephesians 4:32).

- Prayerfully determine whether you need to actually go to the person or whether it is sufficient to cut the tie and forgive without a face-to-face meeting. If you really do need to ask forgiveness for someone you know you have hurt, resist the temptation to fall back on this. Go to that person and humbly ask forgiveness. It will heal a mountain of pain.

- When you choose "yes" to forgive, let it go. Remind yourself when it rears its ugly head again,

  "This has already been dealt with; this was taken care of at the Cross. I refuse to entertain thoughts of how wronged I was; I refuse to entertain thoughts of that person's betrayal. I have chosen to forgive them and do not ever have to deal with that issue again."

- Ask God to help you forget. Psalm 103:12 says, *"as far as the east is from the west, so far has he removed our transgressions from us."* (NIV) When we realize that God truly has no memory of our sin, it enables us to concentrate our energies on living a godly life and do as He has done. Believing the lie that we are not forgiven and holding on to the pain of unforgiveness drains us of energy. It diverts energy from living the Spirit-filled life. Tell your heart to align with the truth of God's way.

- You may need to let go of your expectations on that person. He or she may not be able to fill your expectations. To hold unforgiveness against them for something they may be literally unable to do or be in your life holds you both back. It can create anger in you when expectations are unmet and can harm the relationship.

- Remember that forgiveness may involve the same person and many offenses resulting in numerous times of forgiveness. In that case, ask God for the gift of forgetfulness. At some point, you may need to re-evaluate the relationship, asking God for clarity.

- Consider whether or not an unhealthy soul tie has been created between you and that person where they or you have the power to manipulate, control or hold sway.

- Remember Romans 12:17-21 which contains the principle, *"Vengeance is Mine, I will repay, says the Lord."* If you seek your own vengeance, God will not seek it on your behalf. And His plan is always better.

- If a person has harmed you and is unavailable, write them a letter (but do *not* mail it) telling them you forgive them for their words, attitudes and actions that wounded and harmed you. Name the offenses. Be specific on how you think they have hurt you. Burn the letter and with it your hurt, anger and unforgiveness.

- If you have wronged them and they are unavailable to where you cannot have a face to face or other access to that person, write a letter *(but do not mail it)* asking them to forgive you, noting specifically what it was that you are asking forgiveness for. Then work it out between you and God. Like Jacob (Genesis 28:10-22), do not let Him go until it is resolved in your heart and you have been able to cut the tie. This is especially helpful if the person has passed or moved on and you do not know where they are. Do not use this method as an excuse not to go to the person and ask for forgiveness if they are available.

I hope you take these things to heart even as God's Spirit reveals more things to you about this that you can place in your weapons' armory.

Certain people in your life are there for the long haul: spouses, children, family, perhaps life-long friends. Chances are pretty good that you will need to forgive them more than once or twice. In this case, plan ahead how you will respond. Not that you are expectantly watching for some offense, but just in case it comes. Be prepared to walk in forgiveness for His sake and because He forgave you. Guard your heart before things happen so you do not fall into unforgiveness and bitterness. Understand the person's way and what hinders them.

174

And do not forget to ask God to show you what part you may play. Be prepared for the mirror to reveal what that person has done to you may be reflected back on you! It may give you deeper insight into the cause of their treatment of you, thus enabling you to forgive more easily and make adjustments in your own life.

One other group some will not be able to forgive is *themselves*. I suggest you take the steps above and apply them to yourself. If you are stuck in your walk, your own inability to believe God's Word on this issue may be holding you back. Repentance (covered in the next chapter) will help you clear the slate. It will then be up to you to receive in faith the forgiveness freely offered.

Forgiveness is part of the process of salvation *(sozo)*, sanctification and wholeness. It gives us relief from bondage to guilt feelings and guilt itself. Though the enemy will always try to pile the guilt on us, whether real or not, we must learn to recognize the difference between true guilt and false guilt. Let the false guilt go and take the true guilt to the Cross. It is a powerful weapon in the believer's armory.

Chapter 23. Mending Tears in the Fabric of the Soul

"If we confess our sins, he is faithful and just and will forgive us our sins and purify us from all unrighteousness." – 1 John 1:9

"Repentance is necessary to receive from God. Continued repentance is necessary to maintain and keep that which God has given." – David Stewart (Ancient Oils of the Bible)

A Repentance Story

Robert Robinson was a gifted preacher, poet and hymn writer who lived in the eighteenth century. Despite having twelve children, his life revealed an unsettledness in soul and ministry. After many years in the pastorate his faith began to drift and wane to the point where he left family and ministry ending up in France living a life of sin and indulgence. One rainy evening as he was walking the streets of Paris in despair, a carriage came up beside him and a beautiful young Parisian socialite who had recently been converted to Christ asked him if he wanted a ride. With no idea where he was going, he said yes. The young woman asked if he was on his way to church and he hesitantly said he was. It was then that she pulled a book of poetry she had been reading out of her purse and asked his opinion. As she read the words to him, *Come thou fount of every blessing, tune my heart to sing thy grace. Streams of mercy never ceasing, call for hymns of loudest praise,* she heard weeping and turned to him in astonishment.

When she asked what was wrong, he told her, *"I wrote that poetry. But now I have drifted away from Him and cannot find my way back."* With the gentle wisdom of God speaking through the young woman, she said, *"Why, don't you see? The way back is written right here in the third line of your poem: 'Streams of mercy never ceasing.' Those streams are flowing over you here tonight."* Those words changed Robinson's life. He recommitted his life to Christ that very night, repenting and confessing his life of sin. Restored by streams of mercy, he went on to pastor a church in England with over a thousand in attendance.

For years Robinson was not able to receive forgiveness, perhaps because he really did not understand the nature of how to receive it or could not believe it was for him. Instead, he wandered through life a despairing and depressed man. Many of us are like that. We do not truly understand God's forgiveness, nor do we understand that living a life of repentance and confession to God brings about a continual fountain of cleansing water in us, enabling us to live in the power life God has purposed for us. In the last chapter we spoke of forgiveness – giving it and receiving it as a weapon of war. How we activate it is described in this chapter.

Repentance and Confession

When I was in the midst of the 2012 journey, I did not fully understand the power of repentance, confession and cleansing as weapons of war either. Throughout my life I had experienced many seasons of it, but it was the most recent experience that was the most powerful – as though in some ways I was super-charged to see differently. I saw and understood that the enemy wanted to keep me from experiencing it or, if I did enter in, to keep it as a ritual rather than a reality, a truth, a force that in my own time and space changed something.

Repentance is an exceptionally powerful weapon of war in the believer's arsenal. It is our repentance and confession of sin that restores relationship with God. When we sin, the relationship is broken. It is only restored when we ask forgiveness and repent. Repentance is also a huge part of spiritual health and wholeness. As we are finding out, even our physical health can be impacted.

What Repentance is and What it is Not

Repentance is an attitude of the heart and an action which confirms the attitude. In the Greek it is the word *metanoeo* which means,

> "To repent with regret accompanied by a true change of heart toward God. To turn around and go the other way".[57]

Mounce describes it this way:

> "A radical, moral turn of the whole person from sin to God. A radical new way of life oriented towards God. Its proof is in the changed thinking of a way of life."[58]

Confession is a speaking of the deed. Confessing our attitudes, actions and words are all part of God's cure to bring wholeness and healing to the soul. Just like our sins are composed of attitudes, actions and words, so too, our heart attitude of repentance involves:

- Our words ("I'm sorry God for ___").
- Our actions (putting aside that which grieves God and captures me).

- Our attitude (sorrow for grieving God).

Repentance accepts full responsibility for our actions, our words and our attitude.

Repentance as an Attitude

We can be very sorry for something we have done, sorry we got caught, sorry for the consequence we might have but still not be repentant towards God. It accomplishes nothing. It sent Judas to hell. Although I may be treading in deep theological waters here, my study of Judas' life tells me that, though he traveled in Jesus' circle as one of His disciples, he never actually placed his trust in Christ as Messiah. He was, however, aware of his sin but nothing in the Scriptures confirms that he repented (*metanoeo*) and moved toward

179

God. Matthew said Judas was sorry and he recognized that he had sinned:

> *"Then Judas, which had betrayed Him, when he saw that He was condemned, **repented himself,** and brought again the thirty pieces of silver to the chief priests and elders, Saying, I have sinned in that I have betrayed the innocent blood. And they said, What is that to us? see thou to that. And he cast down the pieces of silver in the temple, and departed, and went and hanged himself."* – Matthew 27:3-5 (KJV)

The word for "repent" in this section is *metamellomai* (different than *metanoia* described above). This word for repent means:

> *"to…express a mere desire that what is done may be undone, accompanied with regrets or even remorse, but with no effective change of heart. It means little more than a selfish dread of the consequences of what one has done whereas metanoeo means regret and turning away by a change of heart brought about by God's Spirit."*[59]

Like many people, while Judas recognized he was a sinner, he did nothing to change the fact. He never agreed with God that what he had done was sin. Matthew Henry in his commentary says,

> *"He repented himself; that is, he was filled with grief, anguish, and indignation, at himself, when reflecting upon what he had done."*

Godly repentance means to agree with God that what we have done is sin. D.L. Moody defines it this way,

> *"Man is born with his back toward God. When he truly repents, he turns right around and faces God. Repentance is a change of mind. Repentance is the tear in the eye of faith."*

A repentant heart is one that grieves over grieving God and is moved to walk away from that which grieves Him. Judas grieved for himself only. The Bible tells us that *"Godly sorrow leads to repentance"* (2 Corinthians 7:10).

Repentance as an Action

I think of the movie *Fireproof,* as one which so clearly pictures repentance. In the movie, fire fighter Caleb (Kirk Cameron) was having marital problems, largely due to his own selfishness and addiction to pornography. His wife began a flirtation with a doctor she was working with and things began to disintegrate in the marriage. It wasn't until Caleb, at the urging of his father, agreed to take action through a forty-day "Love Dare" challenge that things began to change. At first he was doing the challenge only to please his father and save his marriage. He evidenced no godly repentance but more of a selfish dread of the consequences of losing his wife.

Then, his life made a dramatic turn. In one of the most provocative scenes in the movie, Caleb's porn addiction welled up in him. At a crossroad, he realized his desire for God was greater than his desire for sin. It was even greater than his desire to restore his marriage. His sorrow at having offended God rose up in him and he took his computer into his front yard and threw it to the ground, beating it with a baseball bat. Though it did not immediately change his wife's mind about getting a divorce, he had come to a new place. He had found a place where God was able to work in his soul *no matter what happened.* He had turned from something (his sin, his dreams of a good marriage, his hope of a restored marriage) *to* God. Nothing more. That is a picture of repentance.

Confession is the "Word" Part of Repentance

Confessing sin to God means "to speak the same thing." It is to acknowledge, *"Yes, God. I agree with You that when I (name the sin), it is sin and I am sorry for it."* Whatever attitudes, words, or actions we have committed that grieve God need to be confessed. To deny sin is to deny God's word that "all have sinned" (Romans 6:23) and block His Spirit from working in the soul. Confession not only invites forgiveness but also invites His ongoing work in us. In the next chapter we will look once more at David's life, this time after his sin with Bathsheba.

Chapter 24. Cleansing a Repentant Heart -- A Biblical Story

"Then if my people who are called by my name will humble themselves and pray and seek my face and turn from their wicked ways, I will hear from heaven and will forgive their sins and restore their land." – 2 Chronicles 7:14 (NLT)

"True repentance is to turn over the soil of the heart for a new planting of concepts and directives. It is a vital aspect in the overall sphere of spiritual maturity." - Francis Frangipane

Taking a Deeper Look

David understood the need for confession and repentance in his life, which he wrote about in Psalm 51. He had formerly praised God and walked in faith when he killed Goliath and saw God show up in his life. Like many of us, until God pointed out his sin through the prophet Samuel, David probably did not see. If you review 2 Samuel 11-12, you will understand David's horror when the realization (through the words of the prophet Samuel) fell upon him that his attitudes, actions and words caused a deep rift in his relationship with the God he loved. You have also read my story of how I was able to step back into relationship with Him.

As we are now in restoration and recovery phase, I want us to look at three of David's psalms. The first is Psalm 51, which expresses David's understanding of repentance, cleansing and receiving forgiveness. Psalms 32 and 38, which follow Psalm 51 in time, describe David's life after sin with Bathsheba but before repentance. All are instructive because we see the unveiling of David's joy upon release and forgiveness in Psalm 51. But in keeping with his promise

183

to "instruct transgressors" and show them the way back to God (Psalm 51:12-13), Psalm 32 and Psalm 38 are David's firsthand account of what living without repentance can look like (and feel like) in one's life.

It's time to pull out your journal. Let's begin by reading Psalm 51 and answering the following questions. You are familiar with David's outward (and inward sin) and you are familiar with mine. Let's look at the three psalms and apply them to a scenario from your own life. As you do this exercise, you will understand the deep connection between un-confessed sin and consequence as well as repentance and restoration. The exercise will also help you "step in" to Jesus' footsteps when you have stepped out in any way.

Read Psalm 51

1) What words does David use to request pardon from God for his words, actions and attitudes? (Psalm 51:1-4, 7-9)

2) What words does David use to request forgiveness and restoration? (Psalm 51:2, 10-11, 14-15)

3) What do the verses say about David's understanding of God's character during a time of repentance? (51:1, 4, 6, 14, 16, 17, 19)

4) Turn Psalm 51 into your own private prayer to God for forgiveness and restoration. Don't forget to name the sin(s) you are seeking forgiveness from.

Read Psalm 32

1) What words describe David's understanding of God's character? (32:1-2, 4, 7)

2) What physical characteristics does David describe that occurred as a result of his un-confessed sin (32:3-4)?

3) What steps does David describe as his path to restoration? (32:5-7)

4) In 32:5, What was God's response to David's confession and repentance?

5) In 32:8-11 God is speaking to David. What does He tell David about how to be restored to fellowship?

6) Turn Psalm 32 into a psalm of praise for God's forgiveness toward you.

Read Psalm 38

1) What does David see God doing in his life because of his sin? (38:1-2)

2) What physical characteristics does David describe occurred as a result of his un-confessed sin? (38:3-10 and 22)

3) What soulish consequences does David describe occurred as a result of his un-confessed sin? (38:3-4 and 13-18)

4) What outward consequences did David experience as a result of his sin? (38:11-12)

5) Turn Psalm 38 into a psalm of praise for God's restoration in your own life.

Repentance is tied up with faith. It takes faith to believe you are forgiven and believe that it is done. Because we don't often "feel" differently after confessing, we think it hasn't "taken" and we need to do it again. That would describe me. I often find myself confessing the same sin over and over because I don't "feel" forgiven and nothing had outwardly changed in my life. That is where my faith is little. God's Word says if we confess, we will be forgiven, cleansed and restored. Once again, we come back to the full circle of taking God at His Word. If we truly take God at His Word, we move forward as though the deed is done.

Repentance and Health

I re-read an old book that has been on my library shelves for many years just for this portion of the book. It is called *None of These Diseases*, by S.I. McMillen, M.D.[60] Dr. McMillen was a forerunner in the area of connecting health and wellness with the spiritual life. He saw early on the connection between body health, soul health and sin. Our brief study of Psalm 32 and Psalm 38 speaks of these things as David describes his physical ailments at the same time he was living with his unconfessed sin.

Dr. McMillan tells of a man about forty years old who experienced stomach problems. He could not sleep or work and considered quitting his job. After examining him, the doctor found nothing physically wrong and began to probe further. Finally, the man said, *"I have done things that should put me behind bars."* The doctor told him no medication would help that scenario but that he must "bow his head, confess and ask his Heavenly Father for forgiveness." After humbly bowing, the man had an almost instant recovery. Following up with the man a few years later, the man had not lost a day's work. Dr. McMillan states,

> *"What a person eats is not as important as the bitter spirit, the hates, and the feelings of guilt that eat at him. A dose of baking soda to the stomach will never reach these acids that destroy body, mind and soul."*

The washing and cleansing that comes from repentance and forgiveness are the antidotes to illnesses which begin in the soul and attach to the body. I encourage you to do further work in this area. Start with Dr. McMillan's book. There is an updated version. It will open new vistas in your soul to the possibilities of God's miraculous healing work done in correlation with our own obedience and application of His Word. It is all beginning to make sense to me! I hope we are on the same page.

The Cleansing Agent: The Blood

No one likes to talk about blood unless they're a medical student or a phlebotomist. And that is how the enemy wants things to stay. In the early church a rumor took root that Christians were cannibals because they "ate the body and drank the blood of Christ." If that rumor could take root today, you can be sure the enemy would use it. But he really doesn't need to because the blood of Christ is rarely spoken of (unless in passing) in the churches today. Pastors don't preach it, worship leaders rarely sing of it (thankfully my church is a notable exception to this trend), and few Bible studies focus on it. I read somewhere that several years ago one denomination removed all of the "blood songs" from the hymnal because it scared the children. That wily enemy takes the most potent, powerful and under-used weapon in the entire universe and neutralizes it because most of us do not really understand its power. There is perhaps no greater weapon in our arsenal than the blood of Christ.

While cleansing is the result of our repentance and confession, the cleansing agent is the blood covenant sealed at the Cross by the shedding of Christ's blood. It gives us hope, sets us free and restores the relationship. It is the greatest, most important weapon we have available.

The Old Testament had an elaborate method of ritual cleansing, which is a teacher to show us God's holiness and moral purity. Blood was the purifying agent then just as it is over us now. Called "the New Covenant" or "The Blood Covenant" (Luke 22:20), it was an agreement forged between Jesus Christ and the Father, sealed by the Spirit. The blood of Christ forged the covenant, representing an oath or a promise whereby The Father binds Himself to do certain things for His people upon Christ's completion of His part. Christ promised to live a perfect, sinless life and present His unblemished life to His Father in surrender and as satisfaction for the sins of any and all who would come. With the completion of the blood sacrifice, the Father would pardon every soul seeking forgiveness through the blood. Through the Spirit, Christ's blood set the seal of God's promise on His offer of forgiveness through faith in Christ.

Beloved, there is so much more to the blood covenant than we can take up here. Books have been written and are yet to be written on this subject. Andrew Murray's book *The Blood of the Cross* is a classic on the subject. It has been a part of my library since 1979 though I cannot in all honesty claim to have understood the depths of its teaching until going through this recent journey.

There is power in His blood. His blood cleanses us and makes us righteous. The enemy shudders and flees when he is reminded of the blood. It provides a barrier over which he cannot cross. He has no power when we claim the covering of the blood. You must understand the power of the blood as a weapon of war. Lewis E. Jones in his hymn, *There is Power in the Blood* reminds us of our victory: *Would you o'er evil a victory win? There is wonderful power in the blood.*

Christ's Blood as the Mending Agent

We have already learned that one of the words for salvation is *sozo*. It means, in part, to rescue, deliver, make whole. Our salvation happens as a result of Christ's shedding of blood on the Cross. Let's look at Hebrews 13:20-21 together for a moment because I want you to see the complete circle God's Word gives us to understand what Jesus has done for us:

> *"Now the God of peace, that brought again from the dead our Lord Jesus, that great shepherd of the sheep, through the blood of the everlasting covenant, Make you perfect in every good work to do his will, working in you that which is well-pleasing in his sight, through Jesus Christ; to whom be glory forever and ever. Amen."* (KJV)

These verses tell us that the blood of Christ is what makes us "perfect" in every good work. The word "perfect" in the Greek is *katartizo* which, like *sozo*, has a wealth of meaning. It means to,

> *"Put a thing in its appropriate position; to repair, mend (as in a broken net), to 'set a broken bone', to reunite in mind (as in a broken relationship), to restore or set a broken bone or an out*

of joint limb, to adjust, to equip an army for battle, to fit perfectly."[61]

Every one of these meanings has power to change everything in us. When you consider every word above stated as referring to the blood, you will understand. The blood of Christ puts things in their appropriate positions; the blood of Christ repairs my soul; the blood of Christ mends, unites and restores broken relationships with Him and others; it equips us for battle. It mends the broken things in my life. Wow! When we understand the blood, we are placed in a proper position of power to claim it, to use it to mend broken hearts, restore relationships, revive broken bones, call forth limbs out of joint and command them to reset. We also have power to equip others and ourselves for battle.

Beloved, do not, no not ever take the blood of Christ for granted. Do not underestimate its power to change everything and do not ignore the power of this weapon in our arsenal. Every drop was bought with the greatest price. Every drop of blood cost the Father everything He most loved to bring to Himself everyone He did not want to live without in eternity.

Andrew Murray says,

> *"Be assured that if God tells you the blood of His Son cleanses you from all sin, that is the truth. The blood has a supernatural, heavenly, divine power to cover and blot out sin before God immediately and forever...Humble yourself before God, that the Holy Spirit may apply it to you and cleanse your heart by it. Simply believe in that blood as shed for you. The Almighty God is faithful and will accept you for the sake of the blood. Jesus will cleanse you by His blood and will work out in you the cleansing and impart to you the joy and power which the blood alone can bestow."*[62]

Having just read Psalms 32, you saw in verse three that when David kept silent about his sin, failing to confess or repent, his "bones wasted away" because of his sin. His confession and subsequent cleansing cleared that up. His bones were "mended". It is through the blood that our brokenness (body, soul, spirit) and our relationships and the challenges in our life are "set right". We are made perfect by the blood of Christ. The tears in our soul, the health of our bones, the ability to stand firm against the enemy all are made possible through the blood of Christ. The blood has been supplied. It is time for the blood to be applied.

The blood of Christ has bought us:

- Forgiveness – Hebrews 9:22
- Redemption – Ephesians 1:7, Hebrews 9:12
- Deliverance from an old way of living – 1 Peter 1:19
- Intimate relationship with God – Ephesians 2:3
- Peace with God – Colossians 1:20
- Freedom from sin's binding power – Hebrews 9:14
- Purity – 1 John 1:7
- Freedom from sin – Revelation 1:5

I will confess to you that I barely understood the power of the blood even though I sang about it as a young adult. It was not until I went through the process of restoration we are talking of in this book, that I could see it more clearly. When I realized how much sin and unforgiveness was in me (and still is in me), I wept. As I pictured myself clinging to the splintered wood, sitting beneath the Cross and allowing the beloved blood to fall on me one precious drop at a time, I wept. It was then that the reality and the power really hit me. I still tear up when I think about those moments of intense cleansing and freedom I experienced. There is power in the blood. There is cleansing. It is mine and it is yours. It will never lose its power; it will never run out; it is sufficient for the sin of every sinner. As Murray says, *"Simply believe."*

Chapter 25. Oxygen for the Soul

"Hear O Israel, the Lord is our God, the Lord is one. And you shall love the Lord your God with all your heart and with all your soul and with all your mind." -- Deuteronomy 6:4-5

"Worship is to honor with extravagant love and extreme submission." -- Webster's Dictionary, 1828

True Worship

If there is one thing the enemy is very frightened of it is true worship unless it is directed toward himself (at which point it would not be *true*). Worshiping God is a powerful game-changer for the soul and it took me a long time to get even a glimpse of what it is about. It is an amazing weapon in the believer's arsenal. It is like being given an unending canister of air on a planet where none exists.

My evolution of understanding came in parts. Years ago, I saw that worship is not something we do only on Sunday mornings where we sing and speak praise, although done well, it can assist us in creating an atmosphere for true worship. It is our *words* and more.

More years later, I understood a piece of it from one of those awful moments when God spoke directly to my heart as I griped about the music in our church changing from hymns to contemporary songs. Sitting in church one Sunday morning with arms crossed, head down, grousing to myself, *"How can anyone worship God with all the noise in here!"* I heard the Voice that changed me. He said simply this, *"It's not about you!"* In a flash of insight, I knew God had spoken and He expected me to get the message and readjust my *attitude* to His wavelength. I experienced an immediate and lasting soul shift as a result of that experience. Thank you, Tom Lanning, for assisting God in my attitude change! I understood in an instant that it wasn't *what* you did or the words you used, but it was *the attitude of heart* in the doing of it that mattered to Him. To see me now you would never know that I was once a fusty old bag on Sunday mornings grimacing, with ears covered or worse, coming late to avoid the "worship."

The next thing I learned was that worship is more than words and even attitude. It is also *action-oriented*. It is bringing a meal to someone with an attitude of gratitude toward God that you can do it; it is writing a note of thanks or encouragement to a friend, thus exhibiting a heart like His; it is pulling out your wallet and giving beyond your usual tithe; it is serving Him with your whole heart at whatever task He puts before you, whether it is preaching a sermon, feeding the poor or serving tables. It is to reach up and out to Him for more of His presence. To worship God is to honor Who He is, not for what He can do or what He owns (everything), but for Himself, His beloved character, His qualities, His Presence.

The *shema* (Deuteronomy 6:4-5) is an example of how God taught the Jews to worship Him. It is to love Him with everything in you: your heart, soul, mind and body; it is to obey Him in all and out of your love for Him. It is all about Him; it is all for Him. To worship Him is to surrender to Him with deep love and reverence. As I am standing at the door, I recognize that I cannot even capture what it means to worship Him in spirit and truth as Jesus told the woman at the well. She was better able than I to see, to hear, to understand and to follow in this area.

And some of you are like me in this. I have been known to raise holy hands with tears streaming down my face in church on Sunday morning only to criticize and tear something or someone apart on Sunday afternoon. And I know I am not alone in this confession! But God also knows that my heart was genuinely for Him on Sunday morning and, when I repented on Sunday afternoon, He knew that my regret and sorrow over my unruly tongue was also authentic.

Beloved, we are but dust and the enemy loves to eat our dust. So I somehow sandwich my sin between acts of worship (praise and repentance). It does not excuse my sin and reveals to me parts of my heart that are still stony, but God knows my feebleness and that I do want Him more than I want to sin. So I praise Him on Sunday morning and I repent on Sunday afternoon. In a way, both are elements of worship in the midst of a rugged, seedy life that needs more of Jesus.

So, with what little understanding I have, I offer the lessons and thoughts I have learned along the way in the hope that it will spur you on to seeing and maybe seeking worship differently.

Worship is Celebration

The word "worship" in Hebrew means to "bow" or to prostrate oneself before a deity in order to do him honor and reverence, specifically to bow before God. In Greek the word *proskuneo* means to kiss the hand toward or by kneeling before. The meanings don't speak to me. Our culture does not kiss the hand or bow before so we do not get the real flavor from the meanings. But one thing I am learning is that I know it when I am in worship, exalting God above all. His Presence falls. There is a sense of holiness that comes over us as in being in God's presence or a feeling of fire coming over a person or a group that is truly worshiping Him. I have seen it and I have been a part of it. I want to experience more of it. I want my life services to be in homage and service to the One I love.

It can also mean to serve. Ungers says, *"It is as natural to worship as it is to live."* In its fullest meaning it is to reverence, trust, love, be deeply loyal and fully dependent on the one loved. Keil says worship is a necessity of the human soul. *"We were made for worship."* There is something implanted in the soul of every person that must worship something or someone. If we suppress the truth about God and refuse Him, we will find something or someone else to worship. It is part of our humanity. (Romans 1)

Worship is an action word. We cannot sit passively in the pew and wait for God's Presence to fall on us. We must call out and reach out to Him. When we do, whether it is reaching out in your spirit or with hands high, or falling on your face before Him because you cannot receive one more drop of His goodness, He joins you. Years ago I heard the words to the song *Breathe* by Michael W. Smith, *"I'm desperate for You…"* This song captures the flavor of true worship for me. I was and am desperate for more of Him.

Practical Aspects of Worship

Worship God for Himself alone with no agenda for self because He is the lover of our souls. He is the magnanimous, gift-giving God. He may give us unexpected gifts in worship. I often perceive that He moves from person to person during worship whispering different aspects of His Name, depending on the need. *"I Am your Deliverer; I Am your rescuer; I am your Shepherd, I Am your Provider."* The Bible teaches that worshiping God brings His presence into our midst. Psalm 22:3 says,

> *"He inhabits the praises of His people."*

The New Testament counterpart is Matthew 18:20,

> *"For where two or three have gathered together in My Name, there I am in their midst."*

I have seen people healed during worship times. God has also touched me deeply in my soul during worship. Often when I go into worship, I will take a troubled or sick friend with me in prayer (not physically present). For example, if I know of someone who is fighting cancer or heart disease or dealing with a troubled marriage or a troubled child, I pray over them even as I am praising God and thanking Him through corporate worship (as in church) or private worship when I am alone. As I sing or pray and bow, acknowledging who God is, I will bring that person's name before the throne as though they were there with me. I expect God to touch them. I often pray for those around me, asking for their needs to be addressed. There is power in worship, and prayer is often super-charged during these times of true worship.

As we move on to the next chapter, I want to give you a Biblical illustration of worship, the heart of Jesus' message for all.

Chapter 26. The Heart of Worship -- Jesus' Message

"And Solomon, my son, learn to know the God of your ancestors intimately. Worship and serve him with your whole heart and a willing mind. For the LORD sees every heart and knows every plan and thought. If you seek him, you will find him. But if you forsake him, he will reject you forever." -- 1 Chronicles 28:9 (NLT)

"I'm coming back to the heart of worship where it's all about you, it's all about you Jesus." – Matt Redman

It's All for Him

When we offer our worship to God, we are inviting Him to inspect our heart and soul for anything that is not of Him. We invite Him to expose in us the true condition of the heart. That is what happened to the woman in John 4. She met Jesus at the well and He invited her to have a conversation with Him. Let's take a look at that section of Scripture. Read John 4:4-42, then let's talk.

Most of us have been taught that this section of Scripture is about how to "witness for Christ" and how Jesus led this woman in conversation to a saving knowledge about who He is. When we next hear the teaching or come upon this section in our reading, we tend to gloss over it thinking, *"I already know this one."* That would describe me. I do believe that the witnessing aspect is a huge lesson in this story, but as I am moving further on in my journey of the soul I also see it as an amazing lesson in understanding true worship. Just encountering Jesus at the well brought forth profound questions in the woman's own soul about worship, questions I still ponder in my own life. So I hope that as we look at this section, you will be open to a deeper understanding of what He is still doing in the lives of His beloved people through this portion of Scripture. The onion lives on![63]

Jesus, in leaving Judea for Galilee could have taken one of three routes. The most direct route was through Samaria, but Jews usually avoided that route because of a long-standing hatred toward the Samaritans. Samaritans were a mixed people, part Jew and part Gentile, which went back generations to the Assyrian captivity in 727 B.C. Because Samaritans could not prove their genealogy as true Jews, they were shunned. They set up their own religious system and temple, which caused even more prejudice against them. But Jesus had a divine appointment that day. He sent the disciples off to buy food while He sat by the well. Scholars are divided on whether He arrived at the well at noon (Jewish time) or six p.m. (Roman time).[64] But whatever time He arrived, no one else appeared to be there and He was weary, thirsty and hungry. He was fully God and fully man.

Not long after sending the disciples off, a Samaritan woman approached the well. No self-respecting Jew would speak to a Samaritan or a woman. Some Jews were even known to avoid speaking to their own wives if they were seen walking on the same street. I know what I would have to say about that custom! But Jesus was on assignment from the Father. He was the first to speak:

> *[Jesus] "Give me a drink." [Woman] "How is it that you, a Jew would speak to me?"* – John 4:7-9

When Jesus begins a dialogue with someone, whether it is you, me or the woman at the well, He has a purpose in speaking. In this instance, He asks a service of her. It is how He forms character in us, by asking our assistance, by giving us an assignment. It brings us into fellowship and community with Him. We become fellow-workers with Him (1 Corinthians 3:9). In this instance, it is His opening dialogue toward reaching the woman's soul. She is astonished at His speaking to her. She does not know to Whom she speaks. That is about to change. When she entered into the conversation, she gave Him unspoken permission to enter into her soul and expose it to her:

> [Jesus:] "If you knew the gift of God; and if you knew who it is that asks you for a drink, you would ask for living water and He would give it to you." [Woman:] "Sir, you have nothing to draw with and the well is deep. Where do you get this water? You aren't greater than our fathers, are you?" –John 4:10-12

By His answer, Jesus caused *her* to thirst. Jesus touched her soul by telling her that living water could be hers for the asking, but she did not understand, thinking He was speaking about literal water. But she was nonetheless caught by the conversation. Beloved, God's gift of living water, that which enables us to worship Him fully is available for the asking. In the Greek, "gift" refers to an honorable, beautiful, free gift. Mounce says,

> "Water was viewed as a precious gift from God, turning the dead earth into a fertile land by means of a surging spring of mayim (water)."[65]

It is what Jesus does for the soul. He calls it *living water.*

- It has a life all its own.
- It is the source of life.
- It never runs out.
- It constantly bubbles up and satisfies the deepest thirst.
- We cannot live fully without it.
- Drinking it turns a dead, dry soul into a fertile continent, able to create space for the God of the universe to enter in.

We need physical water to thrive physically and we need spiritual water to thrive spiritually. The gift is found in the depths of the well – the soul. It is God's answer to the misery resident in every soul, whether His already or whether still to be won for Him. There is a craving in each of us for water, physical and spiritual.

I am currently on a health journey. I am working with a nutritionist, Garret, who assists me in living healthier. I have always enjoyed good health, but as I am growing older, I have become aware of how much I have taken that good health for granted. I have not eaten well for much of my life and have, over the last few years, become convicted that my "temple" needs work!

The first thing I did was answer a lengthy questionnaire about my life habits, not just food. After reviewing, the first thing Garret told me was, *"You are dehydrated."* I balked at that, completely caught by surprise. *"That's impossible. I drink over a gallon of water a day and have done so for several years."* Being rather proud of that accomplishment, I was stunned when he said,

> *"Nevertheless, you are dehydrated. You are not absorbing fatty acids or minerals. So the water does not absorb fully in your body. It just runs through, often taking needed nutrients with it. That is why you have thirst, cravings and do not sleep well."*

I needed water, yet I was constantly drinking it! There is a spiritual component here that I want you to see. Like my physical journey toward wellness, we may think we are spiritually thriving when, in fact, we may be dehydrated for the living water of the soul.

As Jesus was speaking to the woman, He was speaking about salvation, but as you and I already know, salvation goes beyond accepting Christ and continues on with us in our journey. *Sozo*, one of the words for salvation, means healing of the soul, rescue, wholeness, deliverance and a healthy spirit. These are all promises we have already addressed. This is just one more picture from the Word that God gives to us to confirm and express that abundant living, refreshment, restoration and revitalization comes from Jesus living deep within the well of our souls. It happens when we worship.

200

> [Jesus:] *"Everyone who drinks from this water will thirst again. But whoever drinks the water I give will never thirst. The water I give shall become a well of water springing up in him (his soul) to eternal life."* [Woman:] *"Sir, give me this water so I won't be thirsty again or have to come all the way here to draw water."* – John 4:13-14

I want you to see that Jesus is telling the woman that the water He gives is soul water. It springs up "in him" (the person receiving the water) and brings about eternal life. The gift is available but we must ask for it. The woman was blind to the One offering her the gift, but she still asked for it. Now *she* is the one who is thirsty. She was in His presence but could not see. She is not unlike those of us who have suffered a gouging out of our own eyes at the feet of the enemy. But Jesus Christ comes to restore sight and give sight to those who do not see. He comes to free those who are caught. And she is caught. Look at how He speaks to the woman.

> *"Whoever drinks the water I give will never thirst. The water will reside in you, a never ending well springing up from within."*

Okay. Sign me up!

> [Jesus:] *"Go call your husband."* [Woman:] *"I have no husband."* [Jesus:] *"You have told the truth for you have had five husbands and the one you now have is not your husband."* [Woman:] *"Sir, I perceive that you are a prophet. Our fathers worshiped in this mountain, and you say that in Jerusalem is the place where men ought to worship."* – John 4:16-20

But there is a catch. Before the woman can receive the water, her sin issue must be addressed. *"Go call your husband."* As we have already discussed in earlier chapters, our sin stands in the way of fellowship with Him. When we come to Christ, we learn that our sin, not the part but the whole, was taken care of once and for all at the Cross.

Totally forgiven! But even after salvation, sin continues to dog us and affect our relationship with Him. This is where repentance and cleansing come in to play. We are forgiven, but the fact of our ongoing sin still stains us and keeps us from community with God and others. Therefore, for our own good it must be dealt with. We cannot receive the continual bubbling up of the living water of abundance until our sin is addressed, whether at the beginning of our salvation journey or in the midst of it.

The woman's sin revealed to Jesus a picture of her thirsty soul. Jesus pointed out the number of men she had been involved with, opening to her that she was trying to fulfill her deep thirst within at the wrong well. We will *never* find satisfaction in the soul by all of the different activities we come up with to fill the emptiness. Only He can fulfill the void. Our actions are often mirrors to our soul, expressing our longings and thirsts. We latch on to things that do not last. It's time to pull out your journal here and dialogue with me on this question, looking into your own soul. What things do you fill up your life with hoping to find satisfaction? Sex, drugs, alcohol, eating, TV, shopping, video games to name a few are often things that can reveal our own attempts to satisfy our emptiness.

These areas express our longing and desire for true worship, but until the sin issue is addressed, true worship does not take place.

In this story her spiritual satisfaction and thirst depended on her dealing with the issues that kept her from drinking and absorbing the water. Just like my water journey, in order to absorb the water properly, I had to take the right path to healing. In the woman's situation, no one enters God's presence without cleansing in the way God prescribed it. We have already learned this. It is where we began our salvation journey, receiving forgiveness for our sin.

I want you to notice how Jesus revealed her sin but did not stay in it. *"I know you sinned; you know you sinned. Let's move on."* Done. He covered the bases but not always the same way in every life. There was repentance as we will see later, but it was not evident from this section. He called out her sin in the gentlest of ways, waiting to see how she would respond or if she would respond. It sounds like she was shutting down the conversation and subsequently changing the subject with her flat statement, *"I have no husband"*. However, Jesus saw something different. When He continued the conversation, He told her the truth about herself and the fact that she has had five husbands and the current man she was with is not her husband. She did not continue to obscure the truth. Her thirst overrode her shame.

A turning point took place here. She was not changing the subject. Many scholars agree with me, though not all. Some of what I researched said that the woman's statement showed an unwillingness to be drawn in to personal matters, but her next words, and I paraphrase, can also be seen as a cry for help:

> *"Well, WHERE do I go to worship? Where can I make a sin offering to be cleansed from my sin? How do I worship? You say Jerusalem and our fathers say our mountain. How do I get some needed help here?"*

Is that not the cry of every soul? Where can I go for help? Who will save me? How do I get clean? If she were just raising a smokescreen theology discussion, Jesus would not have answered her question. Instead, He saw into the soul. It is not unlike Nicodemus' cry in the prior chapter, *"then how can one be born again?"* (John 3:9) Only in this case, the issue blocking the truth is sin and how to get free to worship. She had a deep heart's desire to worship but did not know how or where. This piece is close to your heart and mine. We have loved Him; we know Him; we want more of Him:

> *"How do I get more living water in my soul?"*

Jesus loved to be with sinners, not so He could join them in their revelry but so He could break down chains, win them from their ways, pour grace on them and send them on in freedom. My former pastor Mark Hopper used to say, *"Come as you are but don't stay that way."* Christ doesn't condone our sin but He enters into the pain of stuckness in it. He doesn't join us in our carousing, but He is with us nonetheless. He comes to lead us out and He doesn't just do it once, but over and over as we repent, surrender and submit in sincerity to His guidance. He sets the captives free and for many of us it happens more than once, in fact, many, many times. But not once do the damning words, *"Oh it's you again"* come from His mouth. He sees, He frees and we step back in.

> *[Jesus:] "Woman, believe me an hour is coming when neither in this mountain, nor in Jerusalem, shall you worship the Father. You worship that which you do not know; we worship that which we know, for salvation proceeds from the Jews."* – John 4:21-22

Jesus revealed to the woman that worship does not just happen in a place. He kept her on track by telling her that the real key to worship comes from within where true worship takes place. The fact that your fathers worshiped in a certain place or a certain way is not the issue. Worship is an inward attitude. While Jesus confirmed that salvation is from the Jews, it was not because they were better but because He Himself, the Messiah was a Jew. He alone is the one who saves. I think it is extraordinary that Jesus shared such truths with a Samaritan and a woman. But He gives her even more insights, two important ones.

> *[Jesus:] "The hour is coming and now is when true worshipers shall worship the Father in spirit and truth. For such people the Father seeks. For God is Spirit and those who worship Him must worship in spirit and truth."* – John 4:23-24

Jesus told the woman two very important points about worship in this verse. He told her how to worship and why we worship in this way. Then He told her the magnificent results of engaging in true worship. It takes my breath away!

204

Worship in Spirit and Truth

"True worshipers shall worship the Father in spirit and truth." Jesus is telling the woman here that worship is the highest, deepest, noblest part of our humanity. It is where we reach out to God with the depth of who we really are. We are to worship Him in "spirit and truth" because He is spirit. It is His nature. Notice the word "spirit" does not refer to the Holy Spirit, but to our spirit. We worship Him "in spirit".

Worship involves worshiping the Father with the Spirit (residing in our spirit) and with the truth. "Truth" here does not just mean worshiping in genuine sincerity – it also means worshiping in Christ. In John 14:6 Jesus told the disciples, *"I am the way, the truth and the life. No one comes to the Father but through Me."* So then, Jesus created the amazing picture of worship for the woman: You worship the Father through Me (the Son) by way of your spirit (where My Spirit dwells). What Jesus told the woman means that worship is done in the deepest part of who we are in community with all of the Godhead. We not only worship Him. We worship *with* Him. Wow! Who knew? And who knew how powerful a weapon worship really is? Can you see it?

God is Seeking out True Worshipers

"For such people (true worshipers) the Father seeks." How did I miss this one? He tells her the Father is the One who seeks out true worshipers. Precious ones, we do not seek Him. He seeks us!

> *O let me be found worshiping; let me have days and months and years with Your presence in my midst; do not flee from my presence because I am an ungrateful grumbler – O help me in the deepest part of who I am to worship You in spirit and in truth!*

We can learn much about worship through reading the Old Testament. We learn from Psalm 22:3 that He inhabits the praises of His people. We learn from Psalm 65:1, a Davidic psalm that, *"Praise awaits you, O God, in Zion…"* In other words, praise awaits you wherever I am.

When you worship, He finds you. He is attracted to where true worship is taking place and He joins people who are worshiping. When we approach in humility, with bended knee, lifted hand and open heart to embrace Him through our praise, He will join us because He is always seeking worshipers.

> *[Woman:] "I know that Messiah is coming (He who is called Christ); when that One comes, He will declare all things to us." [Jesus:] "I who speak to you, I am (He)."* – John 4:25-26

As God wooed this woman who was in deep pain, she moved from seeking fulfillment in others to finding it in God alone. It is right here that the human soul truly begins to change and enter into God's holy place. As she found fulfillment in God, He began to remove from her the insecurities, the shame, the pain of being unwanted and unloved and the heartaches that life had conveyed to her.

She knew and understood that the Messiah was coming – One who would declare all things. And then Jesus, Messiah, the Holy One of Israel brought the truth to a lowly, lonely, abused street woman. *"I who speak to you, I am (He)."* He tells a society throwaway His name: *"I AM."* What a Savior! What a lover of this lonely, lowly God-seeker. I almost cannot contain the truth of it! And neither could the woman. She was so excited, she left her water jug, her own soul now fully satisfied, and literally ran to the city (some distance away) to share the gift with all who would listen. It was to the *men* she spoke. They knew her story. The group might have included those who might not want their involvement with her known. If there really was someone who knew all things, better to go and find out the scoop. No matter how they came, the change in her was too amazing not to see something was afoot.

Watch the progression here. This is how they knew what she was saying was true: she no longer needed to hide her sin. Her shame was undone, her soul cleansed. She was new, different, and alive for the first time. She was shouting the truth in the streets.

> *"Come, see a man who told me all the things I have done. Is He not the Christ?"*[66] -- John 4:29

This was action-oriented worship. Her attitude changed, her words declared the truth, and the deepest part of her was undone and open for all to see. And, because of what they saw, all who heard her ran to see for themselves. In 4:39-42, they began to believe after hearing her story (verse 39), but in verse 41 many more believed because of Jesus' words. And finally, in verse 42 these lowly, shunned, hated Samaritans were given the gift of sight and insight. Not only did they believe for themselves, but they believed Him to be the *Savior of the world*. Oh, what a mighty God we serve. He is One who stoops to the lowest to reveal holy secrets, unimaginable truths, mysterious workings.

Beloved, Jesus is still in want of what we alone can give. It is our humility and surrender, which satisfies His soul and opens the door for His Spirit to breathe and work. This woman knew He had a real thirst. For what Jew would ever drink from the cup of a Samaritan or a woman? In the beginning she misunderstood the nature of His thirst. His thirst came from the depths of His own spirit to heal her broken soul and bring her to newness. And with that, His own soul was satisfied. He taught her a new kind of worship, one that was done in spirit and in truth. He engaged her in communion with the whole of the Godhead – not in a place, not outwardly but inwardly.

One of the continuing themes in this book is that all of us, every part, every cell, every breath, and every moment is involved in living life for Him. First, we saw that our sin and our subsequent repentance are made of up our attitudes, actions and words. And now, when we come to worship, it too includes our attitudes, actions and words.

Beloved, this journey of the soul – the continual stepping out and stepping back in is hopefully a forward movement with occasional lapses that occur less often as we grow closer to Him. As we have seen in this book, growth happens in the soul. As more space in the soul is created through His healing power, our obedience, warring in the Spirit and our worship of Him, becomes more and more in the forefront of the journey.

The power of worship is so much stronger than we know. All of the weapons God has given us in His Word are so powerful and so useful for different circumstances. But worship is something that is useful in *every* circumstance. Like Michael W. Smith's song,

> *[Breathe:] "This is the air I breathe, this is the air I breathe. Your holy presence living in me. This is my daily bread; this is my daily bread, Your very Word spoken to me. And I'm desperate for You and I'm lost without You."*[67]

Along with prayer, worship is like breathing. It provides oxygen for the soul.

Chapter 27. Secret Weapons in God's Armory

"Remember that you were slaves in Egypt and that the Lord your God brought you out of there with a mighty hand and an outstretched arm. Therefore the Lord your God has commanded you to observe the Sabbath day." -- Deuteronomy 5:15

"Praise is a declaration, a victory cry proclaiming faith to stand firm in the place God has given you...Praise declares that you will not be moved by the enemy's attempt to snatch you away."
-- Darlene Zschech

Illustration from History

Christiaan Huygens was a 17th century clock maker who invented the pendulum clock. One night while lying in bed, he noticed the pendulum clocks in his collection that were sharing a wall were all swinging in unison. He didn't set them that way. He got up and reset them so they would all be out of sync with one another. After a short while, they were all swinging in unison again with each other. It was later discovered that the largest clock with the strongest rhythm pulled all of the other clocks into sync with itself. This is called entrainment.

The heart is stronger than the brain. Scientists tell us that the heart, with its powerful magnetic field, is 5000 times stronger than the brain. The heart, you may recall is made up of the mind, will and emotions mysteriously knit together. The heart can hijack the thoughts from the brain and bring it into the pendulum motion of what are called "entry emotions" or core emotions. Gratitude is an entry emotion; thanksgiving is an entry emotion. Instead of the brain's programmed emotions of fear, grief, anger, anxiety, depression and frustration, the heart can entrain or bring these other emotions into sync with whatever core emotions are cultivated.

In a study done by the Institute of Heart Math, discussed in Dr. Caroline Leaf's book *Switch on Your Brain*[68], it was found that negative feelings can be reversed by feelings of love, joy, appreciation and gratitude. Researchers found that HIV positive patients who had positive thoughts and feelings had 300,000 times more resistance to the disease than those without the positive feelings. The Bible has been right all along:

> *"Above all else, guard your heart, for it is the wellspring of life."* -- Proverbs 4:23

Dr. Leaf also gives more insight into the above story:

> *"The debate in science is between the mind being what the brain does versus the brain doing the bidding of the mind. The position you adopt will impact how you view free will and choice."*

The first position, she says, is scientifically and biblically incorrect. Instead,

> *"Our mind is designed to control the body of which the brain is a part, not the other way around."*

As I've thought about this and tested this theory in my own life, it adds a new level to my own thinking about reframing. It also reminds me of the importance of worshiping and praising God in everything. For me, this was an important piece of the puzzle. Core feelings of gratitude, joy, peace and love increase synchronization and coherence in the heart rhythm patterns, which decrease stress. When you have been addicted to negative thinking like I have for much of your life, it takes more than a strong will and a desire for change to turn that lifestyle around. We could probably say that about most addictions.

Praise and Thanksgiving

One thing I began to do as I was trying to change my thinking was to read the psalms, turn them into prayers of thanksgiving, and use them to acknowledge God's character. For example, read Psalm 57 then read my prayer version:

> *"Thank You that you are the merciful God and that You have mercy on me; thank You that in You my soul has a place to come for refuge and rest; thank You that in You I have a safe place to wait until disasters pass me by; You are God most High; You are One who keeps Your promises and fulfills Your purposes in me; You are the one Who saves me; You are the One who is faithful; You are the one Who loves me. Be exalted O God, let Your glory be over all the earth. Thank You that You have given me a steadfast heart that will stand firm in any situation; to You I will sing and make music. Awaken my soul to You Lord and I will praise Your Name; thank You that You give me the power to speak of You to those I meet; Great are You, Lord. Great is Your love and Your faithfulness to me. Be exalted, O God. Thank You that Your glory is over the earth."*

The more praise and thanksgiving I input into my soul, the more my words, thoughts and actions will align with Him. There is a lot to re-organize in my soul and I have many days, like today for example, that I do not "feel" like praising Him or doing much of anything else either. These are the important days – the days when, even if I don't feel like doing something, that my actually *doing something* changes things.

I learned about praise mostly from following in David's footsteps. As I read about his life, how he approached God, I saw why God loved him so much. I began to pray through the psalms and, in doing so, learned many praise words and phrases that I could send

211

heavenward. As I saw how thankful David was, I began to thank God for *something* even if I didn't feel like it:

> *"Thank you for my house; thank you for my garden; thank you for my family and friends; thank you that I have another day of life to praise you; thank you for the blood of Christ; thank you for the sacrifice of Christ; thank you for the Helper; thank you that your plans for me are good; thank you that you are a good Father and that you love me."*

Just writing these words has lifted my soul.

I've read a lot of books but there are only a few I have read more than once. Stormie O'Martian's, *The Prayer That Changes Everything* is one of those. I have read it over more than once because in it I have learned the importance of praising Him in the midst of my own darkness:

> *"Whenever we express our love for God through praise and worship, we open up the channel through which His loves flows into our heart. We invite His presence to come into our lives in a powerful way that, in the process, breaks down the strongholds of negative emotions. That is the hidden power of praising God."* [69]

It is worship and praise that invites Him into our souls. That speaks so loudly to me because it reminds me that I am not alone in the journey from spiritual warfare to spiritual wholeness. When I consciously invite His presence into my soul, the enemy cannot stand. He must flee.

Fasting as a Weapon of War

John Wesley said,

> *"Some have exalted religious fasting beyond all Scripture and reason; and others have utterly disregarded it."*

Fasting is not talked about much, though I have noticed in the nutritional world it is being more talked about for its health benefits. There is that. But more than that, it is a powerful spiritual weapon. It is mentioned 25 times in the NIV Bible.

Jesus fasted during His temptation in the desert and He taught the disciples that fasting is an important element of spiritual warfare (Matthew 17:20-21). Other Biblical people who fasted include Moses, Elijah, Esther, David, Daniel, Paul and others. Note that every name listed is by now familiar to most of you. That says something about the spiritual power of fasting doesn't it? Down through the ages men and women of deep spiritual faith and ministry fasted. Martin Luther, John Calvin, John Wesley, Jonathan Edwards, Charles Finney and many others. To those intercessors who pray over nations and kingdoms today, it is common and often is used in conjunction with prayer. I'm convinced one of my best friends, Vicky Eagleson, who is an intercessor, fasts more often than she eats. She says it supercharges prayer. I believe her.

Examining your motive for fasting is an important consideration for beginning a fast. Sometimes I have other ulterior motives, like losing weight or other nutritional reasons. A true fast must solely center on God and be initiated by Him for a specific purpose. I confess, I'm not a good fast-er. However, there was a moment in my life when I clearly heard God's voice commanding me to fast. I instantly entered the fast.

About two years ago, while finding my way back to God and preparing for a retreat, my husband became ill with heart issues requiring several surgeries. In one particular incident, he said he was not feeling positive about the surgery. Driving down the street one morning he shared his veiled concerns about coming through the surgery. At that moment, I felt the elbow of the Spirit nudging me. *"You need to fast. Now."* From that moment and for the 21 days following, I entered into a Daniel Fast (Daniel 1:12). It was probably one of the most powerful things I have ever done. My husband recovered completely and the retreat was an amazing blessing to all involved, and became the catalyst for this book. I have fasted for shorter periods since that time, but have not experienced the direct force of God's nudge since that time. Even without the nudge, however, there is power in fasting when it is done with pure motives.

Richard Foster in *Celebration of Discipline* says that there are different benefits from fasting.

> *"More than any other Discipline, fasting reveals the things that control us...Anger, bitterness, jealousy, strife, fear – if they are within us, they will surface during fasting. At first we will rationalize that our anger is due to hunger; then we will realize that we are angry because the spirit of anger is within us."*[70]

There are various ways of fasting – from all food, certain foods, certain things (think TV, cell phones, Facebook), or for certain purposes: Clarity to hear God's Voice; while praying over major decisions. Consider fasting for a friend or family member who is ill; pray for national or world concerns.

As you continue to grow your arsenal, make sure that fasting is a central part of your weapons armory.

Friends, do you see how many weapons we have at our disposal that cause the enemy to flee? I am not saying he doesn't leave his residue behind which we need to clean up through continued partnership with God, but at least, while we are learning how to praise and thank God, his presence is not welcome and he is not doing more damage. I am comforted by that. I am making progress and, as you input these weapons into your life, so are you.

Chapter 28. The Power of Remembering

"Remember the wonders he has performed, his miracles and rulings he has given..." – Psalms 105:5 (NLT)

"Life is wasted if we do not grasp the glory of the cross, cherish it for the treasure that it is, and cling to it as the highest price of every pleasure and deepest comfort in every pain. What was once foolishness to us – a crucified God – must become our wisdom and our power and our only boast in this world." – John Piper

Altar Points -- *Remember*

Right along with praise and thanksgiving, the Bible instructs us to "remember" and to do things in "remembrance". These are words God used often to instruct His people. The word "remember" is used over 240 times in the *New American Standard Bible*. The past, for good or evil, can shape our present and our future. We need to "turn things around" and reframe them. Remembering God's goodness is one way to do that. Remembering His past works in our life is more than an invitation by God to remember; it is a call to identify with and be shaped by His work and action in our lives in those moments. There is healing in remembering how He showed up at "just the right time"; or answered a prayer in a miraculous way; or remembering how different life was before Christ.

In the Old Testament God gave His people instructions to "remember" and He provided different ways to remember His acts. Mostly God gave those instructions so that His people would teach their children the stories so their faith might grow, but also for their own faith to grow. It is a weapon of war that helps us in times of darkness. As God builds pillars of His presence into our own lives, as we share those stories with our children, and others, their faith is strengthened and we are reminded about Who He is and Whose we are.

I call these moments in life *altar points*. They are times to remember when God showed up. If you do not keep a journal of these moments and events, I encourage you to use whatever medium works for you (art, some kind of photography, a memory box, a shadowbox, a video) to help you remember God-sightings throughout your life as God answered an important prayer or even something more dramatic. Be creative in this process and always date things. You think in those moments you will never forget, but I have found that not to be the case. I am grateful that I have a journal to help me remember God's manifestation in my life at so many points. When I am an ungrateful wretch, whining and complaining, I only need to think about or go to my journals of past days:

> *Remember when He healed your back the day before you were to speak at a retreat? Remember when funds came in unexpectedly when you were not able to pay the mortgage? Remember when He restored your ability to imagine? Remember in college when you needed a certain piece of music and a stranger showed up having just what you needed – then you could not find her to thank her? (or was it an angel?)*

All these things and more are my altar points. They are there to remind me and our family that He is with us. These are the days, moments and years of living a life of faith with Jesus. And as you grow closer to Him, the moments become regular happenings rather than just once in a lifetime sacred doings.

The Jews had many God-sightings throughout their history. The Scripture records these events when God did something extraordinary and the Jews built altars to memorialize them. (Like in Genesis 8:20, 12:7). They would utilize other methods of remembering as well:

216

- **Stack up stones**: *"Take up twelve stones from here out of the middle of the Jordan, from the place where the priests' feet are standing firm and lay them down... Let this be a sign so that when your children ask later...these stones shall become a memorial..."* (Joshua 4:1-7).

- **Sew "memorial stones"**: These stones were sewn onto the priests' garments so when they and the people saw them, they would remember God (Exodus 28:12).

- **Sew tassels into clothing:** The Lord instructed His people to sew on the tassels to remind them of God's commands, *"...that you may obey them and not prostitute yourselves by going after the lust of your eyes and heart"* (Numbers 15:37-40).

- **Place blood over the doorposts:** God told them to do this while they were still in Egypt so they would remember later that His angel "passed over" them in judgment when he saw the blood (Exodus 12:23-24).

- **Acknowledge the feast days and celebrations:** God told them to remember Him and His care through the feast days and celebrations, including Passover (Exodus 23:14-19; Exodus 13:1-10).

- **Remember the Sabbath:** God commanded them through the Ten Commandments written on stone tablets to, *"Remember the Sabbath and keep it holy"* (Exodus 20:8, Deuteronomy 5:15).

Many altars were built to remind people that the way to redemption or forgiveness is sprinkled with the blood of the acceptable offering. We celebrate communion in *"remembrance of Him"* whose blood was shed on the Cross and as the only way to wholeness. Through communion we identify with the crucifixion and we remember that we started our walk with God through the sacrificial offering of His Son.

Scripture tells us that remembering God's movement in our lives can help us "stand firm" against fear. Nehemiah 4:14 says the people were nearly overcome with fear and discouragement, but Nehemiah helped them to stand firm and fight:

> *"When I saw their fear, I rose and spoke to the nobles, the officials and the rest of the people, 'Do not be afraid of them;* **remember the Lord** *who is great and awesome, and fight for your brothers, your sons, your daughters, your wives and your houses.'"*

In Psalm 77:11-12, the psalmist attempted to calm his fears and the fears of the people by remembering:

> *"I shall remember the deeds of the Lord; surely I will remember Thy wonders of old. I will meditate on all Thy works and muse on Thy deeds."*

Remembering is a powerful weapon in the armory of God's weapons.

Keeping the Sabbath

"Remember the Sabbath day by keeping it holy."—Exodus 20:8

Sabbath is a God-given pattern for living. When we are observing the Sabbath in some way, we are imitators of God who created, then rested. The Hebrew word *Sabbath* means "cessation", to cease, to stop. On every Sabbath the Levites sang Psalm 92. Mounce says this about the Jewish Sabbath:

> *"The Sabbath was a time of celebration at home with feasting, the inviting of guests, and special blessings closing the day. It was also a time for worship in the temple or synagogue."*[71]

For Christ-followers it also has the sense of trust – resting in His plans for us because He is a good Father. As we let God's Word and His Spirit lead us to the solutions He has already provided, we find rest in Him.

Sabbath is a weapon of war because observing it aligns us with God who rested after creation. When we rest in His presence, enjoying the rest He commands for our own good, we are more likely to stand firm. It increases our resources by increasing strength for battle.

John and I have become more aware of enjoying and celebrating the Sabbath over the last year or so. We have taken a twenty-four hour period from the week (not necessarily Sunday, though it usually turns out that way) to rest, enjoy faith, family and friends and spend the time reminding ourselves of what rest is for and then *doing it*.

One of the favorite ways to celebrate is to invite a group of friends, a couple or some singles over on Friday or Saturday evening *after dinner* to enjoy post dinner appetizers with us on the deck. If I have the stress of cooking a large meal for guests every week, I won't do it, but I can handle heating up an appetizer and making lemonade or iced tea. Sometimes we take communion and pray together. Perhaps one of us comes up with a one word topic to discuss such as *remember, alter point, worship or even Why Sabbath?* Sometimes we listen to music, play a game or simply watch the sunset or stargaze in companionable silence. For me it is the joy of celebrating God and His goodness with good friends or family members. It gives me great joy to be with people, some who know each other well, or sometimes friends from out of town who join us with friends from here.

Other times, we meet friends at a half-way point, usually near the beach for lunch or early dinner and sit and watch the sunset together. It is the sacred time spent together speaking about God's goodness, and enjoying God's rest with others. Even lunch with a good friend can be a Sabbath rest. Occasionally I will have opportunities to spend a small block of time with a good friend in praise and worship. It refreshes us both to simultaneously lift up holy hands in thanksgiving. For me, being with His people is one way of worshiping the Creator.

There are so many ways to keep the Sabbath. Gordon MacDonald in his book *The Life God Blesses* says on Sundays he welcomes the secrets of God; he contemplates creation; he himself creates according to his gifting or he enjoys others' creations through art, music, or reading a novel.

To me, while Sabbath is not a vacation, it feels like one – a stay away from the ordinary day to celebrate and remember Who God is. I try to put aside worry, anxiety and regrets. I don't think about tomorrow. Instead, I try to revel in today and be thankful that I have family, friends, and a place to have people come. In a 2015 journal entry I wrote:

> *"I am praying and trying to see what a Sabbath might look like in our lives. We have had the benefit of two weekends with our good friends, the Eaglesons over the last month to help us fashion it. Just being with them has been a Sabbath rest. I see some elements coming together: Fellowship on some level; food prepared together or purchased out; conversation; prayer, maybe communion and singing; something special or out of the ordinary – something we would not normally do; rest in being together, joy in who God is and what He invites us to enter into with Him; a sense of listening and watching for how God wants to gift us in the time."*

Make it fit your lifestyle and family system, but try taking time out to celebrate it. It is a weapon of refreshment, something to look forward to, and I am sure you already know the enemy will try to steal it from you. Stand firm! You need this.

There are so many weapons of war. Really, we are just getting started! I hope you will research and check out *celebration* as a weapon. Celebrating the feast days of Israel or even the holy days on the Christian calendar are all ways, if done in grace not as works, that will increase your strength. It will help you remember He is with you.

Also, consider attitude weapons like *surrender, obedience, humility.* There are hundreds. My purpose was not to create an exhaustive treatise on the subject. Other authors with more understanding and maturity have written about these subjects. I hope you will search them out. My purpose is to help you get started, help you see, open your eyes to the truth that we must armor up and take the things God has made available to us to help us stand firm in the journey. To do so means a surrendering or giving all to Him for His use and His glory.

> *"The surrendered life recognizes that it is God's prerogative to choose our place, be it eminent or obscure; to select our task, be it important or insignificant...it is the human surrender that releases the divine power. 'I gave Him everything.' said David Livingstone, 'It is a pity I have so little to give...but no gift is small if God owns it.'"* -- John McBeath from *His Glorious Indwelling*[72]

Chapter 29. Dirt Disasters --A Parable of Our Day

"As the deer pants for the water brooks, So my soul pants for Thee, O God. My soul thirsts for God, for the living God." – Psalm 42:1-2a

"I have learned to kiss the waves that throw me against the Rock of Ages." – C.H. Spurgeon

The Farmer's Garden

Once there was a farmer who planted a garden. It was to be a wondrous thing of beauty and nourishment. It was to feed the farmer's family, friends and neighbors. But the garden had many enemies, foes who wanted to destroy the plantings or eat them before they could produce food for the farmer's family. The farmer planned for all of these things. He began by building huge wooden beds so the plants would have a safe environment to grow in; he even put wire meshing underneath each bed so animals who lived in the dark underground recesses beneath the garden could not burrow in and eat the young plants.

With a great, heaving effort the farmer was able to bring water to the garden. He made sure that every one of the fledging plants would get its own drink of water whenever needed. The farmer reinforced the garden by placing a fence around it so enemies above ground could not get at the tender shoots. Then, because the farmer knew that good dirt is the most important part of the garden, he had dirt delivered, mixed just right for a garden to grow. Just to make sure that all was in readiness, he mixed in organic fertilizer and other special ingredients that he was informed would help the garden grow and be healthier for his family. But even with all of these things, the farmer knew that enemies hid even in the good dirt, waiting in the darkness for the right moment to birth evil on the plants. The farmer was learning that, while evil was hidden in the depths of the dirt, these things too could be addressed when they became known. The plants could even be protected from these opportunistic organisms living in the soil's core. The farmer was learning how.

Finally, after looking over the garden, he determined that it was ready for planting. So the farmer painstakingly planted 127 small seedlings in the garden and waited with great expectancy for the results.

A few weeks after planting the garden, the farmer was called away on a business trip. When he returned several days later, he walked into the garden with great anticipation, hoping to see his seedlings sprouting up tall and healthy. But what he saw greatly dismayed him. Not a single plant was thriving! Some had died and the green leaves of the rest had turned yellow. This sight left him upset and perplexed. What had gone wrong?

The farmer called the company that had delivered the dirt only to discover that no one knew exactly what kind of dirt they had delivered. One employee said it was sod dirt, another it was compost. Only the company's owner would know for sure but he was not available. The farmer even called on experts to help him figure out what was wrong and several helpful people gave him advice. But no one except the owner of the dirt company could fix the dirt problem. The farmer was becoming anxious as the growing season was progressing.

Finally, the owner arrived and immediately sized-up the problem. The dirt consisted entirely of fibers, filler and sand. It contained no nutrients. He said,

> *"Nothing will grow in this dirt. This dirt alone is not good dirt for the garden. It cannot hold water or nutrients. If left,*

everything will die of malnutrition or dry up for lack of water. But if I bring you some dirt with life in it, we can mix some of this soil with the soil I will give you and it will come alive and begin to grow. And every season, as you learn to amend the soil, these plants and other new plants will thrive. **Then you will see the garden do its miracle!"**

And the owner was good on his word. After the new dirt was poured in and mixed with some of the old dirt, the plants that had survived were re-planted and thrived over the seasons. The garden gave and still gives good food to the farmer, his family and friends.

The Meaning of the Parable

If you haven't figured it out by now, this is one of my garden stories. This really happened close to the way I have written it. I cannot seem to write parables the way Jesus told them, so as I explain it, some pieces will not fit. For example, the owner of the dirt company represents God. He is the only one who can fix the problem and bring in new, better dirt to the soil of our souls. But the God of my life never makes mistakes. He is perfect in all of His ways and knows intimately every micron of "dirt" in every garden. And He is always with me. His timing is always perfect. He is the only One who can fix the problem and He is the One who can diagnose any "dirt" problem in any life.

The dirt itself is a picture of the soul. Before God comes on the scene, the soul's dirt is like the lifeless dirt described above. It can hold no nutrients and no water. Nothing planted can grow into wholeness. But when we come to Christ, new dirt is poured into our soul through truth and the promises He gives such as righteousness, the power of His blood, the armor and more. Things begin to happen in the dark recesses of the soul. When the water of the Holy Spirit begins to hydrate the dirt and pours the living water in, even more things happen.

225

The plants or seedlings represent the truth: imputing truth into our souls through reading the Word and seeking deeper communion with Him through prayer and worship. There are endless ways to receive truth. Seedlings planted in the right soil prepared for them will flourish and grow, providing us food in its season.

The enemies of the garden reside under, outside of, or in the soil of the soul. They burrow into our lives to kill, steal and destroy the plants planted in the soil of the soul. They are there to snatch the seedlings before they take root. We have talked about numerous ways the enemy comes to kill, steal, destroy and rob of us of the truth. He uses outside influences to attract us and things already resident in the soul like traumas, wounds, sin, negative patterns, habits and addictions.

In Luke 21:34-36 Jesus says,

> *"Be on guard, that your hearts may not be weighted down with dissipation and drunkenness and the worries of life, and that day come on you suddenly like a trap; for it will come upon all those who dwell on the face of all the earth. But keep on the alert at all times, praying in order that you may have strength to escape all these things that are about to take place, and to stand before the Son of Man."*

Just as I must constantly be on the alert for possible invasions from within, without and under the ground in the garden, so we too must be alert in our souls. Waiting too long to deal with these things or not keeping watch can be devastating to the garden and the soul too.

About the same time the garden disaster was occurring, I was reading about Gideon in my Chronological Bible. I began to focus on his journey from orphan-hood to stepping into his God-given identity. I also began to look at the weapons of war God gave him. In the next chapter we will look at one this final Biblical example of how God brings us through to victory.

226

Chapter 30. Orphan's Journey to True Identity -- Bible Story

"The Lord is with you, O Valiant warrior." – Judges 6:12

"This was not just a man threshing wheat; it was God painting some above ground imagery for Gideon (and us) to see." – Priscilla Shirer

A Lesson in Seeing what God Sees

Let's start by doing a brief walk-through of Gideon's life. The story begins with Gideon hiding from the Midianites on the threshing floor. By failing to join in the battle for freedom for the country, Gideon had in some ways stepped out. He did not see who he was or what he could do to help win the battle. Believe me, I know we could do a whole book on Gideon's life alone, but let me highlight some important points as they relate to our topic of *stepping out and stepping in*. Read Judges 6:11-18 and Judges 7, then let's talk.

The following quote is from my journal of April 5, 2015:

> *"I have always loved the angel's view of Gideon in Judges 6:12 when he called out, 'The Lord is with you, O mighty man of valor.' I picture Gideon furtively looking around to see who the mighty man of valor was who joined him on the threshing floor. It did not seem to describe Gideon, hiding out from the enemy. But God is not bound by who Gideon appeared to be. God always sees beyond, calling forth from each of us something we do not even see or realize lies within us.*

> *Gideon looked like a terrified farmer, but God created him for so much more! Gideon needed a reboot – God had told Him*

*who he was (mighty man of valor) and that He was **with** him, but he needed to see and understand that the One leading him to his place of purpose was able. As a result of those two things, in the strength he had (Judges 6:14), he would deliver Israel. God had to bring him out of the shadows of who he thought he was, into God's light so he could get a burst of reality. Gideon's orphan spirit told him that he was fearful, incompetent, ungifted, worthless, rejected, the least of these and insignificant. But God's image of Gideon was far different. He saw that Gideon was courageous, capable, equipped, valuable, accepted and special."*

And so He sees you and me. Do not let the enemy's lies bury you on the threshing floor when you were meant for more! I hope you have learned this as you have journeyed with me through the book. I hope you are now standing tall, embracing your birthright and seeking your purpose.

As we learn to look at our lives and life in general from God's perspective, we learn to operate from who and what God sees rather than from how the enemy sees as he tries to steal God's viewpoint from us. We must trust God and walk the way He sees us to gain spiritual victory.

Gideon focused on his weaknesses, not realizing that his weaknesses were really his strengths. This is how we experience His presence and His strength. God turns things around and opens doors at the very point of our inability and weakness.

In Judges 6:14, when God told him he would lead the army to victory, Gideon, even after calling on all of his family and the surrounding Israelite community, was still the underdog, gathering 32,000 Israelite foot soldiers versus 135,000 Midianites *on camels*. The odds were against him 40:1. Gideon was hugely outnumbered but, by focusing on his weakness and the disparity of the troops, he was sure to fail. We look at our situation, our resources, our abilities and we throw up our hands in defeat. 32,000 men should have been sufficient to alleviate Gideon's fears and quell his insecurities, but it did not. Gideon's faith in this instance was imperfect. He doubted. So he placed a fleece – or two (Judges 6:36ff) and God was faithful in responding to Gideon's weak faith and saw the fleece as an opportunity to strengthen it.

When God told Gideon that 32,000 were too many soldiers to fight the 135,000 Midianites (on camels), failure seemed even more likely. Gideon reluctantly sent home soldiers as God commanded him to do. Finally, the number was right, from 32,000 to 300 (Judges 7:7). Well that's different! And that also changed the balance of the battle significantly. Gideon's army went from 40:1 to 450:1. Now, without God's help, failure would be a 100% certainty.

God's Weapons

But even stranger were the weapons God provided to Gideon and his emaciated army (Judges 7:15-18). Armed for battle with a torch, trumpets and a clay jar or pitcher, the army marched on. Foolish weapons of war in so many ways, but not one man wavered and God gave them the victory. Beloved, God's ways are not our ways. His weapons are not our choice of weapons. His odds are not what we would even consider … But God!

Let's look at those weapons for just a moment. Read Judges 7:15-22. The jars of clay contained the lit torches, easily hidden by the clay jars. The clay jars were fragile, easily breakable, hiding the light and fire until just the right moment. Note that it was the content of the jars (coupled with the sound of the trumpets) that would win the battle. The jar itself was weak, frail and easily breakable with the ability to shatter easily. Hmmm. Sounds like me and maybe you. But what our jars contain – oh my! It is the light, fire and power of the Holy Spirit residing within us. When our broken lives are surrendered to Him available for the breaking and shattering for His purposes, there is power! And when His light shines in our hearts, the enemy cannot stand (2 Corinthians 4:6-7).

Using God's Weapons, God's Way

When I began walking the journey of the dirt disaster, I tried to utilize my own strength, my natural talents, my legal skills and my own thinking patterns to try to resolve this issue. I called the company every day asking when the owner was coming out and for each rebuff, I got more and more discouraged on the one hand and more angry on the other. Even knowing I would never sue him, I had some comfort in doing it my way. I began developing my legal strategy, calling on "dirt experts" and others to "set up the case". I did this, "in case God didn't show up." O me of little faith!

During this time I was quite discouraged even as I realized that the visible garden disaster underscored the invisible spiritual war going on around me and in me. While I wanted to stand firm in this journey and employ God's weapons, the enemy was tugging me by the ear, trying to tell me it was useless; reminding me that I was alone in the journey and that it was all up to me (I had not yet dealt with the orphan spirit spoken of in an earlier chapter).

In spite of the barrage I was hearing from the enemy, I sat firmly, every morning praying and turning my heart toward Him. Beloved, when you choose to fight your battles in the natural, you will miss the spiritual realities surrounding you. Your victory, if you have one, will have been wrought with stress not peace; pride not humility; discouragement not power. My journal is full of the word "discouraged" during the days of the dirt disaster.

Finally, after about ten days of trying to make thing happen, I wrote in my journal:

> *"I cry out for deliverance and turn my face willfully toward Him – with varying amounts of success – or not. But I will not give up or give in because I know thankfulness incarnates faith*

in the sovereign goodness of God. I will not give up or give in to the enemy."

That same day I walked to the grieving garden, raised my hands in praise and started praising and thanking God. I gave Him praise for creating a place where good vegetables could grow; I gave Him praise that He is the one who fights our battles; that He is mighty to defend; that He is a refuge and strength in time of trouble. I thanked him for our helper and my husband who made such an amazing garden for our food to grow; I thanked Him for the dirt company and asked God to bless them whether or not they responded. I repented of my unbelief (again!). I humbled myself before God telling Him there was no way I could do this in my own strength. I gave up my plans for legal victory. I stood firmly on His solid ground and thanked Him in the midst. I told him I would share the bounty from the garden with those in need. I determined to stand in peace, not anxiousness or discouragement.

The next day the owner came, looked at the dirt, owned the disaster as his own, and determined to make it right. Not every battle you and I are employed in will result in such a quick and major victory, but the success or failure (from our viewpoint) of the situation is not our problem. It is God's and He will stand faithful even when we do not. His purposes and plans will not go awry and He will bring about His solution if we stand in faith and do not go our own way.

It was as I prayed the solution, thanking Him whether or not the man made repairs and recognizing if he did not, God had another way of solving the problem that things began to shift. Learn how to pray the solution, not the problem. Learn to praise Him in **all** things; learn to bow down in humility before Him and, as a gift to Him, surrender yourself. It is in surrender and humility that He moves through our lives. If our pride stands tall and in the way, He will allow us to attempt our own problem solving and will not intervene. It is as we call out to *Abba, daddy* that His ear perks up and He moves heaven and earth to send His solution.

I can think of no better way to end this book than to speak to you of surrender and humility. It is perhaps for us the most difficult part of the journey. We do not surrender well and humility often feels like being a doormat. Nothing could be further from the truth. These are powerful weapons that cause God to move in close and strengthen us even more.

Humility

Humility is the opposite of pride. Whereas pride puffs up and focuses on self, humility focuses on others and God. We do not really like the word humility because it sounds weak and spineless. But that is not what the word means. In explaining the different words for humility, Richards explains that one word, **Anah** (Hebrew) really means, "*To bow down, gentle, submission, force.*" He says,

> "*The force may be exerted by someone who is hostile or by God, who uses affliction to encourage His people to turn to Him.*"[3]

Peter says,

> "*Humble yourself under the mighty hand of God that He may exalt you at the proper time.*" – 1 Peter 5:6

What Peter means here is to face the pain of self-examination, repent and confess your sins. We have already covered this in a previous chapter. True humility is looking into your soul, allowing God's Spirit to reveal to heal and crying out for deliverance to God through repentance and confession. It is fasting and praying and looking to Him for His guidance. It is a recognition and a willing decision to be fully dependent on God for His care and His provision. I can live with that, even though I do not always choose to stay in that zone.

Another word for humility is **kana**. This word suggests a public defeat or humiliation such as is mentioned in 2 Kings 22:19-20. King

Josiah had a humble heart. He was eight years old when he became King of Judah. It was during his reign that the lost book (book of the law) was found. It had been buried and hidden from the people because of their rebellion. When the book was read to the eight-year-old king, he tore his clothes in grief saying, "Great is the LORD's anger that burns against us because our fathers have not obeyed the words of this book." (2 Kings 22:13) Then he ordered the priests to consult Huldah the prophetess. She told them that God's anger was publically and openly on His people for their rebellion, but of Josiah, she said,

> "...because your heart was tender and you **humbled yourself** before the Lord when you heard what I spoke against this place and against its inhabitants...I truly have heard you...therefore, I will gather you to your fathers and you shall be gathered to your grave in peace, neither shall your eyes see all the evil which I will bring on this place." – 2 Kings 22:19-20

And King Josiah lived a long life, making some mistakes, but still living under God's blessing for his humility.

Of course, the best example of humility is Jesus our Lord. He lived a life completely dependent upon His Father, waiting on Him in all things. Even though He had the power of the universe at His fingertips, He humbled Himself for our sake. He suffered a public defeat, but so much more. In Philippians 2:5-11 He willingly laid aside His privileges as God. He emptied Himself choosing to take on the form of a slave for our sake. He humbled Himself to the point of death on a Cross for our sake. And in Philippians 2:9 we see that God highly exalted Him giving Him the Name that is above all names.

There is something mystical, hidden, even heroic about humility. When we are in the presence of a humble person, there is something different about the person which is not easily grasped by those of us who are filled with pride. My son, my husband and I all saw it in our current pastor. It is what made us want to return. After one visit, we wanted to be close to those who attended this church. We wanted to support this pastor, pray for him, let his pain and humility rub off on us. It is his journey, his story, the pain he endured and continues to endure that brings tears to my eyes, prayers for him in my heart, and almost a willingness to take on his burdens. Here is one man who is literally dependent on God for his every breath: a picture of humility. And many of the pastors and leaders there are like him in their service. *"As the king goes, so goes the nation"* is how I teach the concept. If you have a humble king (a pastor, boss, leader or teacher), those under him or her will likely follow in their ways. And you too are a "king" in someone else's life. Learn the lesson well, my friend.

Humility is not being a doormat, but being a willing dependent, not on others, but solely on God. Who really knew? Who really can understand that this is the way of the Cross? We read it, we see it, but we find it so hard to live it. Yet God sustains the humble. In Psalm 147:6, He exalts and blesses those who truly throw themselves on His mercy and care.

It is a way of life I crave even though I find it difficult to achieve. One step at a time -- that is all He asks, and He will not lead me where He cannot keep me. This I know!

Surrender

I have saved this subject for last, perhaps because I am still in the process of learning what it means to "surrender all." As a young adult, I knew I was not fully surrendered even though I desired it. I could not even sing it in the hymns back then. But I am learning and I am willing, or at least willing to be made willing. I was hoping my Bible Dictionary companions through the writing of this book would offer some light, but surprisingly, it was not mentioned in any of the dictionaries I own. That is because, while the concept is there, the word itself is not.

In Matthew 16:24-25 Jesus said, *"If any man would come after me, let him deny himself, take up his cross and follow Me."* The word for "follow" in the Greek is *akoloutheo*, which means self-denial. It means to disown and renounce self and to subjugate **all** works, interests and enjoyment to another's leadership. The Christian walk is not a halfway effort. When you put your faith in Christ, it is a journey and a giving up. But the giving up comes with a promise of His presence with us. That presence is so amazing, so divine, so incredible that it is hard to understand how we could we not want it.

Surrender is tied up with God's sovereignty and our trust issues. You cannot surrender to someone you cannot trust unless you are forced to, which God would never do. If you are uncomfortable with a doctor who is going to perform surgery on you, you most likely would change doctors. If you got on a bus and saw the open flask of alcohol on the bus driver's lap, you would most likely get off at the next stop or before. You would not choose to surrender yourself or put yourself under the power of these people. But with God, it is a whole different situation!

I often read biographies to find out what lessons I can learn to deepen my own walk. One common thread I have seen with those we would consider giants of the faith was their deepening need and desire to surrender all to God as they moved forward in their own journeys of faith. What deeply impressed me about each of these people was that, even prior to their surrender, they had what most would consider "successful ministries." They were leading people to Christ, writing books, music and more. But there was a longing, almost a knowing, that there was more to life than they were experiencing, which is exactly how I felt. Their stories tell of their prayer journey toward "more"; their commitment to go before the Lord and not let Him go until He blessed them with the deeper life.

Surrender leads to the abundant life. That is the missing key. It is the journey toward abundant life. It is what this book is about --following after Him and reaching out for an ever-increasingly deeper experience with Him. Read with me these quotes from some of the men and women of God who sought hard after the abundant life Jesus promises:

- **William Booth (1829-1912) (founder of The Salvation Army):** *"The Holy Spirit has continually shown me that my real welfare for time and eternity depended upon the surrender of myself to the services of God."* He goes on to tell that this was a journey, *"a long controversy"* the end of which, *"are recorded indelibly on my memory"*.

- **D.L. Moody (1837-1899) (evangelist who reportedly preached to over 100 million people during his lifetime):** God used two women from his congregation, who prayed without ceasing for him to receive the Spirit's anointing. After hearing them pray he said, *"I really felt that I did not want to live if I could not have this power for service."* He surrendered, sought God and said, *"I was praying all the time that God would fill me with His Spirit."* When God answered his prayers for more he said that he did nothing different than he had before. *"The sermons were not different; I did not present new truths; and yet hundreds were converted."* And yet his own journey was never the same, filled over and over with increasing opportunities to touch the lost and bless the saved.

- **Francis Ridley Havergal (1836-1879) (Songwriter, Author):** She was a woman who loved God deeply and served Him for many years in many different ways. She lived a *"very earnest Christian life and sought to glorify God and serve Him."* But even with her successes and opportunities to serve, she longed for a deeper Christian experience. She felt she kept falling back into the "dark places" in seeking for more. Her sister later wrote of her, *"She was gratefully conscious of having for many years loved the Lord and delighted in*

His service; but there was in her experience a falling short, not so much of a holy walk and conversation, as of uniform brightness and continuous enjoyment in the Divine life." It wasn't until 1873 when someone sent her a small book, which explained the missing "more" to her that everything changed. Of that time she said, "*One of the intensest moments of my life was when I saw the force of that word, 'cleanseth'. The utterly unexpected and altogether unimagined sense of its fulfillment to me, on simply believing it in its fullness, was just indescribable.*" After that her writings and actions were infused with a new spiritual power. The final years of her life were finished in joy. Her experience was best described in her own words: "*There were strange soul depths, restless, vast, and broad, Unfathomened as the sea. An infinite craving for some infinite stilling; But now Thy perfect love is perfect filling. Lord Jesus Christ, my Lord, my God, Thou, Thou are enough for me.*"[74]

These are just a few of the thousands down through history and those who are alive today who have sought after God with surrendered hearts, ready to give up all for the sake of Him. When God sees that kind of devotion, He is moved to act and bless and move His people to places they never dreamed of, doing things they could never have thought of, reaching heights of mystery so deep that only the One who knows us intimately and loves us unconditionally could take us. And none of them sought for those things – they sought more of Jesus. This is what I want in my life. More of Jesus for the sake of more of Jesus; not to be famous, not to sell books, not to have anything more than a mouth that will praise Him, feet that will deliver peace, hands that will touch people with His power to bring glory and honor to Him alone.

Closing Comments

I leave you with this quote by Walt Whitman which has been such a strength to me:

"Sail forth, steer for the deep waters only, reckless, O soul, exploring. I with Thee and Thou with me. For we are bound where mariner has not yet dared to go, and we will risk the ship, ourselves and all, O my brave soul! O farther, farther soul! O daring joy but safe! Are they not all the seas of God? O farther, farther, sail." – from *A Passage to India*

The following verse also has so much meaning for me. Read this verse, a verse from God's heart to His people the Jews and those (Gentiles such as you and me) grafted in to Him:

"I call heaven and earth to witness against you today, that I have set before you life and death, the blessing and the curse. So choose life in order that you may live, you and your descendants, by loving the Lord your God, by obeying His voice, and by holding fast to Him; for this is your life and the length of your days, that you may live in the land which the Lord swore to your fathers, to Abraham, Isaac and Jacob, to give them." – Deuteronomy 30:19-20

And finally, a verse to you reminding you of Who He is and Whose you are. Make it yours and remember.

"Now to Him who is able to keep you from stumbling, and to make you stand in the presence of His glory blameless with great joy, to the only God our Savior, through Jesus Christ our Lord, be glory, majesty, dominion and authority, before all time and now and forever. Amen." -- Jude 24-25

Sail on! He is with you.

References

1 William Hendriksen, *The New Testament Commentary: The Gospel of Mark*, (Grand Rapids: Baker Book House, 1975), 148

2 William D. Mounce, *The Complete Expository Dictionary of Old and New Testament Words*, (Grand Rapids: The Zondervan Corp., 2006)

3 Spiros Zodhiates, Th.D. ed., *The Complete WordStudy Dictionary New Testament* (Chattanooga, TN: AMG International, Inc., 1991)

4 Zodhiates, Ibid (#2222)

5 Zodhiates, Ibid, (#4053)

6 Craig von Busek, *What are the Three Parts of Man?*, www.CBN.com accessed 7/4/17

7 Kim Laliberte, *The Call to Follow Jesus, Studies in the Gospel of Mark*, (Bloomington, IN: WestBow Press, a Division of Thomas Nelson, 2013)

8 Kenneth Barker, ed., *New International Version Study Bible*, (Grand Rapids:The Zondervan Corp., 1985) 790

9 Francis Frangipane, *The Three Battlegrounds*, (Cedar Rapids: Arrow Publications, 1989) 11

10 W.E.Vine, *Vine's Expository Dictionary of Old and New Testament Words*, (Old Tappan, NJ: Fleming H. Revell Co., 1981)

11 Gleaned from an online talk by Deanna Allen, at www.womensempowermentuniversity.com on Healing and Deliverance. Accessed 4/17/16

12 Jerry Bridges, *Respectable Sins*, (Colorado Springs: NavPress 2007), 17

13 Charles Dickens, *A Christmas Carol* (NY, Tom Doherty & Assoc. 1990), 21

14 Dickens, Ibid.

15 Pastor Mike Reed from a sermon at Calvary Chapel Oceanside, Ca on 8/27/17

16 Lawrence O. Richards, *Expository Dictionary of Bible Words* (Grand Rapids, The Zondervan Company, 1991)

17 Jack and Trisha Frost, *Spiritual Slavery to Sonship* (Shippensburg, PA, Destiny Image Pub., 2016) 37

18 Donna Partow, online classes for women called *Women's Empowerment University*, www.womensempowermentuniversity.com

19 Charles H. Kraft, *Two Hours to Freedom*, (Grand Rapids: Chosen Books, a Division of Baker Publishing Group, 2010)

20 Marilyn Hickey, *Break the Generation Curse*, (Denver: Marilyn Hickey Ministries, 1988)

21 Rabbi K.A. Schneider, *Self Deliverance*, (Bloomington: Chosen Books, a Division of Baker Pub. Co., 2015)

22 Dr. Clay Carlson, Professor at Trinity Christian College, accessed at http://www.trnty.edu/latestnews/1953-080414-epigenetics.html

23 Beth Moore, *Day by Day*, (Nashville:B&H Pub. Group, 2007) 75

[24] Kenneth Barker, ed., *New International Version Reflecting God Study Bible*, (Grand Rapids:The Zondervan Corporation 2000) 507

[25] Richards, Ibid, 207-208

[26] Kim Laliberte, Ibid

[27] Vines, Ibid

[28] Vicky Burke, *Some Days You Dance* (Tulsa:Word and Spirit Pub., 2011)

[29] Zodhiates, Ibid, New Testament Dictionary, 750

[30] Vines, Ibid., 302-303

[31] I am indebted to Dr. Michelle Corral of *Breath of the Spirit Ministries, Yorba Linda, CA* for her teaching on serpents which opened my eyes to this understanding. *Of course* the enemy is like a serpent. His first appearance on *terra firma* was in that form!

[32] www.Titanic-titanic.com

[33] Dr. Barbie Breathitt, *A to Z Dream Symbology Dictionary*, (Richland Hills, TX: Barbie Breathitt Enterprises, Inc. 2015)

[34] Francis Frangipane, *The Shelter of the Most High*, (Lake Mary, Fl:Charisma House, 2008)

[35] Breathitt, Ibid

[36] C.S. Lewis, *Mere Christianity* (NY:The MacMillan Co., 1967)

[37] http://abcnews.go.com/2020/story?id=2918360

[38] Merrill F. Unger, *Unger's Bible Dictionary*, (Chicago:Moody Press, 1979)

[39] Vines, Ibid

[40] Vines Ibid

[41] Ungers. Ibid

[42] Mounce, Ibid, 754

[43] *West's Encyclopedia of American Law*, 2nd ed., (The Gale Group, Inc. 2008)

[44] Walter A. Elwell, ed., *Baker Commentary on the Whole Bible*, (Grand Rapids:Baker Books, a divn. of Baker Book House Co., 1989) 772

[45] E.K. Simpson and F.F. Bruce, *The New International Commentary of the New Testament, (Ephesians and Colossians)* (Grand Rapids, Wm. B. Eerdmans Pub. 1987, 11th printing) 142

[46] Neil T. Anderson and Robert Saucy, *The Common Made Holy*, (Eugene, Or:Harvest House, 1998) 109

[47] Pastor Mike Reed, Taken from a sermon delivered August 13, 2016 at Calvary Chapel Oceanside, (with permission).

[48] Kenneth S. Wuest, *Wuest's Word Studies, Volume III*, (Grand Rapids, MI:Wm. B.Eerdmans Pub.Co. 1975)

[49] Zodhiates, ibid

[50] Wuest, ibid

[51] Zodhaites, Ibid, 950

[52] Maria Durso, *From Your Head to Your Heart: The Change You Long For is 18 Inches Away*, 2015 Maria Durso

[53] Mrs. Charles Cowman, *Streams in the Desert*, (Grand Rapids:Zondervan Publishing Corp., 1996) January 25 reading

References

[54] Dutch Sheets, *Intercessory Prayer,* quoting S.D. Gordon, (Ventura, CA: Regal Books, Ventura CA 1996) 23

[55] Oswald Chambers *Daily Thoughts for Disciples,* (Grand Rapids:Discovery House Pub.) 2/24 devotional

[56] This example provides a visual of what forgiveness looks like. I am not saying that paying 'penance' brings forgiveness. Forgiveness is free and done. Read on!

[57] Zodhiates, Ibid.

[58] Mounce, Ibid.

[59] Zodhiates, Ibid

[60] S.I. McMillan, (Westwood, NJ: Fleming H. Revell, 1968)

[61] Zodhiates, Ibid.

[62] Andrew Murray, *The Blood of the Cross,* (Whitaker House, 1981)

[63] I have said many times that I believe Scripture is like an onion – peeled away layer by layer (often with tears) to teach us to go deeper and deeper into His Word.

[64] M.R. Vincent, *Words Studies in the New Testament, volume 1,*(Florida:MacDonald Pub. Co.) 424

[65] Mounce, Ibid 778

[66] The literal translation in the Greek says, "Is this not the Christ?" Not, "This is not the Christ, is it?"

[67] Michael W. Smith, Lyrics *Breathe,*

[68] Dr. Caroline Leaf, *Switch on Your Brain,* (Grand Rapids: Baker Books, a Division of Baker Pub. Group, 2013) 31

[69] Stormie O'Martian, *The Prayer That Changes Everything,* (Eugene, Or:Harvest House, 2004) 174

[70] Richard Foster, *Celebration of Discipline,* (NY:Harper & Row, San Francisco, 1988)

[71] Mounce, Ibid, 607

[72] Nick Harrison, *His Glorious Indwelling,* (Grand Rapids: The Zondervan Corp. 1988) 309

[73] Richards, Ibid

[74] James Gilchrist Lawson, *Deeper Experiences of Famous Christians,* (New York: Pyramid Books, 1911)

Made in the USA
San Bernardino, CA
11 May 2018